RAISING
BEAN

Made in Michigan Writers Series

GENERAL EDITORS

Michael Delp, Interlochen Center for the Arts
M. L. Liebler, Wayne State University

A complete listing of the books in this series can
be found online at wsupress.wayne.edu.

RAISING BEAN

Essays on Laughing and Loving

W. S. Penn

WAYNE STATE UNIVERSITY PRESS
DETROIT

ISBN 978-0-8143-4930-4 (paperback)
ISBN 978-0-8143-4931-1 (e-book)

Library of Congress Control Number: 2021951019

Publication of this book was made possible by a generous gift from The Meijer Foundation.

These essays represent descriptions of the worldly processes that Clara Bean will encounter, both humorous and more serious. In each, the idea, feeling, or laughter is the main point, and names and characters have been changed or imagined to fit the essay and not the other way around.

Wayne State University Press rests on Waawiyaataanong, also referred to as Detroit, the ancestral and contemporary homeland of the Three Fires Confederacy. These sovereign lands were granted by the Ojibwe, Odawa, Potawatomi, and Wyandot nations, in 1807, through the Treaty of Detroit. Wayne State University Press affirms Indigenous sovereignty and honors all tribes with a connection to Detroit. With our Native neighbors, the press works to advance educational equity and promote a better future for the earth and all people.

Wayne State University Press
Leonard N. Simons Building
4809 Woodward Avenue
Detroit, Michigan 48201-1309

Visit us online at wsupress.wayne.edu.

CONTENTS

Prefatory Remarks

These essays should be seen as being told to my granddaughter, whose nickname is "Bean," an honorific that, in the proper way of nicknames, means an increase (the kind of epithet that insults, denigrates, or decreases is merely a childish insult from a weak mind). As with nicknames, the processes of these essays, I hope, offer an increase of humor, perception, understanding, and thought. They cover a range of ideas and things. "Draining the Swamp" suggests that how a person tells something reveals how and who he or she is. "I Stand Here Listening" (with a play on the great Tillie Olsen title, "I Stand Here Ironing") listens to Clara Bean encounter and consider endemic racism and her innate desire not to participate in it. "Free Love" takes up the idea that there is nothing free about love. "Revelations" is an amusing allegory of anthropologists in the rattlesnake desert revealing how "nature" and "nurture" are not dichotomous or opposed (Rattlesnake remains a rattlesnake and Bumpa remains a bumpa). "A Harvest Moon" introduces the importance of process in stories and in life, and "Not Nobody" suggests the advantages of being Nobody (as Odysseus calls himself), taking note of William Kennedy's comments about the dangers of being "Somebody." Other essays take up the importance of tolerance or the happiness that may come from knowing language and history, the sense that death is not something to fear, and that words, like the opening nicknames, have power, and the utter importance that literature may have in our lives.

Told with a sense of orality the essay/stories are meant to guide, not preach, and to manifest the importance of process over plot. Plots are, to the Native storyteller and essayist, falsehoods. Beyond "He was born, drank coffee, and died," everything we know about people comes out of how they are and how they are remembered. One's birth, in a generational sense, occurs long before one walks the earth; one continues—if loved enough to have stories told about him or her—as long as the stories continue to be told.

Chief Joseph spent long hours sitting beside his lit or unlit campfire, with a world of things passing through his mind. Regardless of how people want to sentimentalize his "I will fight no more forever" speech, given the complexity of the Nez Perce language, they could never have understood. He sat there thinking, like my grandfather sat in a painted Adirondack chair on the porch of a bungalow in Napa, California. He spoke little as his thoughts ranged and connected, bringing together all things, though not all at once. In either case, the connections altered, shifted, changed according to circumstance or need or weather.

What was Joseph to say about General Howard's egotistical pursuit of his band? What makes a person get so consumed by his bureaucratic power and narcissistic sense of personal injury that he wants to repay the Nez Perce sharpshooters for their sharpness and is willing to pretend to treat with Joseph thirty miles from the dotted line that should mean Canadian safety, which a man like Howard might well have crossed if he thought he could get away with it? When Joseph ostensibly says that he "knows General Howard's heart," he is not necessarily saying that he thinks that heart is courageous or honorable; he is saying that he's learned something about these sorts of folks. Were he to tell it in story, he would allow his listener-participant to experience and to learn something about these folks. The need for an underlying humor, however, for avoiding the bitterness that changes nicknames to epithets, may leave either Joseph or Grandfather amused or weary as he enters and exits—contemplates—the weir of words, and leave him silent.

This is for Clara, for you, before I become that.

Acknowledgments

I have to thank some people, people like my agent, Alice Speilburg, for being the best editing agent one could wish for. Annie Martin at WSU Press, whose enthusiasm, generosity, and kindness run to extremes. Emily Nowak, also at WSU Press, whose patience seems to know no bounds, and the tireless copyeditor, Jude Grant, who joined with them to make the book better. Then there are the people like George P. Elliott, Pat O'Donnell, or Arnold Krupat, or Lee Francis who honored me by being friends and colleagues. And finally, of course, my wife, my daughter and son and entire family, who have not only put up with me but also given me great joy.

1

THE POWER OF WORDS—
THEIR USES AND MEANINGS

In the Nick of Names

Names have power. Telling someone your name grants them power over you.

Imagine stepping off a curb crossing against the light because it's raining and getting soaked expands your sense of entitlement enough so that you feel you don't have to obey mundane regressions like signals or crosswalks. Just as you get fully into the first lane (it's a four-lane road), your friend (or enemy) calls out, "Hey, Thom!"

Assuming that your name is "Tom," which your parents purposely misspelled to make you unique, one of only a thousand or so "Thoms" who are not named "Thomas," you pause, hesitate, even stop, only to be flattened abruptly like a cake in the mail by a CATA bus intent on keeping its schedule, which, unable to match your expected entitlement, skids to a halt with its right rear tire crushing your empty noggin.

That's one kind of power.

There's another, deeper power. Knowing your name allows other people to know a lot about you, possibly even to know a good deal about your parents.

Last names, family names, are complicated. They often come from the deepest past. "Burton," for example, may originate with a family that lived on a burr or hill who, because they built no walls to keep out immigrants, ended up not occupying Wall Street but a whole town, a "borough town," which, given the British inability with Shakespearean syllabics, got lazily shortened to "Bur-ton." Others, like Shoemaker or Tailor or Piddler, Smith, or Brown come mainly from historical activities. While Kaashounds are furry dogs who come from cheese lovers or makers, cheesy people names include Kaasbrook, Kaasmann, and Bleukaas who, way back when, got moldy because they were always blue and teary. Kaashole has, over the centuries, evolved to Pyehole as cheese blintzes went to cheese pies to blueberry pie, and finally to four and twenty blackbird pie. Hedkaas remains in use, as there seems to be a lot of those around.

That's all old hat, or Old Felter, most of whom were mad as hatters from mercury poisoning. What about modern names?

Not much has changed. People still fall in and out of love and make war while saying "Make love, not war." They make babies or at least have them constructed and delivered by FedEx and farmed out to care-givers who could give a, well, care.

Oddly enough, the ones who iterate slogans like "Make love, not war" are the very people who think love is constructed and not devel-oped by constant contact and effort. For an example, take a puppy, brought home from the puppy mill to pee and shit all over your plush white carpet until you do one of two things: you successfully house-train it, or you lock it outside where it can poop and pee to its heart's content until winter, at which point you have to make a decision, leave it out to freeze, or hire someone else to train it before your house starts to smell like a rest home with its underpinning of bodily odors faintly hidden beneath the chemical veneer of bleach.

Contemporary people often treat their infants like puppies, say-ing with expectant glee, "We're having a baby." The blank you are. She is pregnant, yes, and she will deliver the bowling ball to the alley in proper measure when it is time. The male of the species sits on his ass or makes frequent trips to the ice chip machine, hopefully during the commercials on Monday night, Tuesday night, Wednesday night, Thursday night, or Friday night football. Saturday is the Sabbath before Superbowl Sunday, and if his wife passes that bowling ball on the Sab-bath, he may want to name it "Sabbath," not knowing that "Sabbath" comes from words that mean "to rest" or "to cease," which is why an American might cease to watch grown (and boy are they, bigger than barns) men give one another head injuries and, failing that, simply cripple them for life (which is called "not staying within yourself").

Anyway, suddenly, there is little Sab (no kid wants to go by "Sab-bath" for fear that he'll start to sound like a dark Goth rock band). You are happy to have its name all chosen—it could be a girl or boy as "Sab" is pretty neutral like "Hay-den" (or "Barn"), "Taylor," "Tinker," "Sol-jure," and "Spie" (which latter is either secretive or hangs red-ily from trees). While the woman ceases and rests, making Sabbath's birthday the only freaking day for the next twenty or thirty years on which she will get to cease doing and rest up, Padre, Daddy, the Mister and Tool of the baby-making trade will change the original diaper, the one filled beyond all diapery measures with a gray goo called meconium; he'll feel all brave and sacrificing in doing it, too.

Now here's the problem, Bean. Names mean. They describe for the rest of the world either a relationship to family or an expectation—accidentally, perhaps—of how that baby may be, the how being vastly more important than what, why, or wherefore.

So if you name your kid "Sabbath," as there is probably no ancestor with a similar name (except Aunt Friday who hangs around oil drum fires outside Yankee Stadium), you should not be surprised if little Sab grows up ceasing and resting and eventually ends up living in your basement when he's forty, with the new puppy. Accidental or not, kids often—with uncanny, innate, and unarticulated purpose—grow up to inhabit their names, to become the meaning their names have given them for all of their available lives.

Sure, "Morts" can grow up to be humorists, but it will be a dark humor, a Jewish humor. The rest will most likely become Morticians (they're fun, the oily floggers of expensive boxes in which to bury what will become worms or, if you are Xtian, dust returned to the great vat of dust hanging about with old Ashes) or Mortgage Bankers gauging your ability to pay usurious sums (again, nice people, but you don't go to your bank dressed to party), or preachers promising ImMortality in the face of climate change or Jim Jones.

In part, at least, growing up to inhabit your name involves the way people respond to the name you hand them to use, in addition to the things you begin to accept as though you know them.

Can LaVapide become anything more than Vapid?

Or how about little Lutheran Zoë whose parents named her Life, after she cuts the cords using the sharp edges of agendas she picks up from the dustbin of schooling, calls herself "Vita," and starts hanging around doing Lucky Charms with Mort? Vita "feels" different (what kid doesn't?) and instead of enduring or surviving the way Life does or ought to do, she finds excuses for why she feels different, forgets that she is not unlike two billion other kids (only a million or so who are actually called "Life," however). She gets angry at her professor because on the first day of class he refers to her as "she" and not "Z." When she leaves and does not come back, she grants new Life to her professor because who the bloody eff wants "Z" in his class who demonstratively insists that the university build special rooms for their alphabets of slight and insult.

The professor's response (oh, not by the U, which wants to pretend to diversify while it doesn't tolerate opinions not in agreement with the common tone and allows or encourages Black kids to all live in the same dormitory so that they won't feel any more uncomfortable than the White kids who would have been their roommates) ought to be like President Obama's grandmother's: "Grow up."

What about the purposefully different names? They often begin with a negative: I do not want my son to be like Uncle Mort who mutters "I'm sorry for your loss" over the Thanksgiving turkey.

I don't want my son to be like me or, worse, like his grandfather whose name I bear, though being like his great-grandfather would be something of a plus. I don't want my daughter or son to wear a name that descends from the assignment of names by slavers to people ripped from their homes and dragged to the New World (which was an awful lot like the Old World, only without cheap labor, or the Present World, which uses hand-wringing as a form of racial justice).

This latter at least has a historical reason. Lots of Indian kids were shunted into the auditoria of Indian schools and, faced with a blackboard listing decent "White" names, were made to pick one. For the parents to want to give them an Indian name that means "Thunder Rising" would be ridiculous only because the child would thereby be condemned to a disproportionate amount of teasing. Parents all want their offspring to be unique, but unique means different, and different can be dire for a kid. Thunder goes around thinking, "I'm unique" when really it is only his name that's unique and he's rather run-of-the-mill which highlights how not-unique he is (there is no "more" or "less" unique; you either are or you aren't).

Maybe a name ought not to try to attempt to create a unique little blob of protoplasm. Maybe a parent seeking a good name for his blob ought to seek connection, place, occurrence.

I mentioned little Sabbath above and made some fun of it, but to recognize the day of the week upon which a child is born is common around the world. Do you know how many African names from a variety of places and countries note that the child was born on a particular day of the week (Aba, Abeeku, Abeena)? So maybe all that is amusing about Sabbath is that it's the quasi-religious aspect of the poor kid's name, fenced into a country in which everybody knows that the Sabbath is on Sunday.

Maybe a name ought to join the child into the swimming ebb and flow of life, ought to grant the child as well as his trusted, name-knowing friend a sense of who he is in the great background of ongoing life, of how we might expect him to be. Martin may be "warlike," but that doesn't mean that the continuous battle he fought had to be violent, and besides, his middle name, "Lothar," meant what he was, a "hero of the people." Dr. King's parents (at least I doubt it) did not sit down and say, "Let's see, we want this baby to be unique so we'll give him a name that is relatively common and undistinguished and only by becoming more, by respecting what he is taught, by enduring and evaluating what he has suffered, will he one day become important enough to get a day named after him." Dr. King's parents had no way to know that he would one day become a "doctor," that through hard work and learning he would teach us all what real oratory and leadership and meaning sound like. But they may have known that having a name like Martin Luther would at the very least make him aware of what can come by nailing ninety-five theses up on the door of a church.

They put "Martin Luther" out there and let him walk right into it, for which we are all grateful, and for which we are all lucky, and for which we need not only understand the power of names but also how the name becomes powerful.

Nowadays, this kind of naming, this who-you-are part of, has been turned on its head. Often, it does not tell who you are (or are becoming) but who your parents hope you may become. Sometimes the thinking behind naming is negative: we don't want little Themba to grow up like Uncle Mort. Moreover, it reveals just how simpleminded your parents may be and whether or not they know how to spell: "Taylor" is still pretty much "Tailor," but "Taylore," with accentuated emphasis on the "lore," means only that your parents are foolish enough to fantasize that misspelling "Taylor" will make you unique, unlike the five hundred other Taylors on the email system of whatever college or junior college to which your lack of "lore" will get you admitted. These are probably people who hear a sportsman or woman talk about "staying within oneself" and think, "Wow, that is right, and so wise," the same people who fall for the trick of tax cuts wherein the rich save a million or two while they save enough to purchase McDonald's milkshakes all around.

"I know, let's name him or her Taylor."

"Great, Bob. Except I don't want her or him growing up to be just like all the other Taylors in the world."

"So how 'bout we stay within ourselves and call it 'Tay-LORE.'"

"Oh, Bob. You're so smart."

"Thanks. And while we're at it, let's take the hundred bucks we saved on taxes and blow it on a splurge at Micky D's."

"You're so sweet. And here I was worried that you'd want to waste it on a yacht or maybe a Learjet or a new window for the front of our travel trailer."

Fewer and fewer young parents don't name their children after blood relations to recognize and acknowledge the fact that you, like me, are not merely a product of people past but also a continuation of them and that it is our individual responsibility to polish the name and keep it bright.

Instead, parents consult lists of athletes, celebrities, or pop stars with the magical hope that little Wilde Bonnet (pronounced "WILL-dah Bone-AY") will naturally, without work or effort, suffering, or endurance, become rich and famous. They try to use the inverted power of names that mean to propel little Wilde Bonnet into the world of success, which they confuse with money—as in "He cheats and lies, but he lives in a tower and has more money than Croesus, so he must be successful"—and without ever questioning whether or not being Midas (the king, not the muffler) is worthwhile, fun, or meaningful.

A name should not be something given or assigned but something acquired. Earned. It's not a gift: "Here, little Taylore, go and be cute and rich"; it cannot express much more than the attitudes of the parents. It's a burden, something that must be lived up to, modified in personal ways, and earned. The name "Taylore" derives, probably, from the occupation of Taylore's forebears, not from an expectation of uniqueness.

What if, growing up, Taylore accidentally reads a book or two that isn't self-help, confessional memoirs, magical beasts, or the possibilities of space travel (and the concurrent possibilities of becoming robotic, a controlled "base" of numbered voters)? What if she, he, or it decides that sh/e/it would rather be happy than rich or that "contented" is not the same as "complacent" or that "noncomplacent" (ah, Diogenes!) might in fact lead into the spa of contentedness? What if sh/e/it actually gets off its butt and leaves the television to go out of the cave and realizes that the shadow on the technological screen is the shadow formed by all the people sitting dumbfounded before Fox News, defined by the light of entertainment and money, and that it is meaningless?

Ought sh/e/it to change its name? Is it even possible for little sh/e/it to change its name? If it has a mind that is mindful, sh/e/it may never again look at Fox News or the shadows of Fox's faithful viewers the same again. It will always be aware of the elusiveness of illusion. Sh/e/it can't change itself by changing its name, but sh/e/it can with effort become something more than s/h/it.

I remember in college in the over-berated sixties, a woman I went out with told me that I ought to go by "Liam."

"Well," I thought, "I am not Irish and I am not Liam."

You can't just change your name and become someone else. No more than you can name someone in the hope that he or she will grow into it. Rather, you inherit (Latin *heres*, "heir") your name and then earn it and make it your own. Else you end up a contradiction caught in a falsehood. Sigurd may name his boy Sigurdsson; if he names him Sigurdssdottir—well, you see the difficulty? If Sigurdssdottir then marries Helgudsdottir, what will they name their son?

"I don't want him to be William the Fourth."

Fair enough. (A numeral isn't going to change things. I mean, so what if Sigurdsson is Sigurdssotherson?) But William he is. We can give him his maternal grandfather's name as a middle name, thereby recognizing the two genetic and moral strains, the Indian and the Italian—and indeed, he will be both.

Like these formal names, "Nick" names are often bestowed out of affection or perception. Nicknames usually represent an aspect of character, a relationship, a modification of meaning among meanings, a recognition of a way of doing things among all ways of doing the same thing, an expression of feeling or thought, an idea or inkling that the name-giver has about the named. Nicknames, in some ways meaning more than formal names themselves, are a gift, given or bestowed as recognition.

Let's consider a racist joke, which is racist primarily because the jokers lack all understanding, like people who fantasize that "stardom" (aka infamy) makes abusing women okay, even permissible. The joke I was forced to hear growing up was about names. An Indian boy pesters his mom to know where he came from. At last, in frustration, she says, "Why do you ask, Broken Rubber?" The joke is an irony of recognition and truth, though it denigrates both. The joke gets repeated by people who do not understand relationships, by people who name their children after Disney Ducks or pop singers as though their children will be automatically infused with pop duckiness.

One way to avoid this is to name your son or daughter after a relative directly in line from the grave: a William is genetically derived from a William and regardless of our fantasy of freedom to become whatever we want to become, our character will still be William, like it or not. He may go by "Willy," but eventually, he will stand before a lecture of five hundred students and hear his father's voice come out of his mouth. He may falter, and if he falters not just because of the fact but also because he doesn't like his father's way of embodying the name William, he must try as hard as he can to go on being William without being his father's William. He, in other words, will go in search of an earned nickname. As "nick" derives from Old English "eaca" and means "an increase," he will be seeking that increase in how he is without suffering the decrease of how he doesn't want to be.

All this, Bean, is a loving, long-winded way of explaining to you your nickname. While "Clara" means "fair," "bright," or "clear," and so far you are, it is also your great-great-grandmother's name, and as a Clara you are expected to live up to and even beyond that recognition of continuity.

While you were hanging about, lollygagging in your mother's euphemistic "tummy," I began calling you "Bean." My reasons for that seem obvious. As our first grandchild, you were the nut around which all future feelings would aggregate.

After you were born, I sometimes called you "Beaner," to which people objected, making me wonder where cultural epithets begin and end and how we determine whether they are "bad" or "good." I'm not stupid or insensitive (I hope). I have been called many things that have to do with "Indian." Where do you think I heard the Broken Rubber joke, from another Indian?

But who bloody cares? People who don't know what words mean use words that don't mean much at all, and why should you or I pay them the respect of attention? Isn't it that feeling that invites some young Black people to use the hateful word "nigger" or "nigga"? Aren't they saying it to each other—and I underscore, *each other*—to suggest that the word in actuality lacks power or meaning? If the slur is intended—and intention does matter—to describe a state of mind or attitude, then, my god, how we're surrounded by a bunch of White, Brown, Yellow, Red, and yes, Black niggers, whoresons who measure "success" by "money."

I imagine a Black person using the word as a way to acknowledge and even laugh at all the people who recoil like the necks of geoducks when they hear the word. I can barely imagine the sheer and overwhelming boredom some Black people must feel about the discussion of the word. Whenever I have been obliged to listen to some theorist go on and on about how "Indian" is a misnomer by men whose GPSs went bad and who, landing in what they thought to be "India" called the Caribbean natives "Indians," I have wanted to dash out of the room, run down the hall, and pee on a potted plant in public.

When I grew up—and where I grew up—the Stanford University mascot was an Indian and the hand-wringing and feelings emoted by the then fledgling political correctors seemed to me—a fat, four-eyed Indian boy—to be much ado about very little. But they changed the mascot, and since there are no staunch defenders of avian rights and feelings, they changed it to something else they considered "red," Cardinals. It—neither the Indian nor the bird nor the color—had anything to do with me, though well-meaning people wanted it to.

Everyone knows Indians don't laugh; we lack all sense of humor, unless we are trying to be good Indians by laughing at Broken Rubber. Second of all, if we grin, it's only as we savagely infest with smallpox the blankets we give out to hurricane victims. Third of all, that feather is all too appropriately an indication of what we think of measuring success by money.

How else can you respond to a country that shifts the originally selected path of an oil pipeline to cut through sacred lands, under a river and lake of Life, in order to bypass the edges of white enclaves of tick-tack houses with eight-foot trees planted in front?

(Wow. Chillax Broken Writer.)

When the Gluten Freedom Riders object to "Beaner," if I claim to be excused because my first sweetheart was Mexican, with real parents really from Mexico who cooked me refried beans, burritos, and quesadillas, I sound an awful lot like some White dude excusing himself by admitting to having one Black friend, of which I have several.

When I was a kid, a person of youthfulness, for me to exclude the colors—the Blacks, Browns, Reds, and Yellows—severely limited the available pool of friends, drained it out, and, like an empty swimming pool, made it dangerous, a concrete hole into which you might fall and hurt yourself. In that particular suburb of the City of Angels (aka White folk), if you didn't team up for kickball on the asphalt field euphemistically called a playground with Blacks, Jews, Mexicans (with maybe a Venezuelan thrown in for diversity), you'd get stuck on a team with Ralphs and Tommys and Donalds, most of whom could only purchase, not play. They could not kick, and if by accident they did, in order to score, they had to dodge rules, not run bases.

You'd lose.

The game.

One thing we colored boys could do was run. Even a fat Red boy like me was taught the focus, endurance, and survival of running. Cars of high-school kids from other worlds drove over after school to hunt us. When our intramural team "traveled" by used bicycle to rival schools to play basketball in cinder-block gyms with accordion bleachers on the sides, we won by margins large enough to let us substitute the Ralphs and Donalds and edge out of the gym early, hopping on our bikes and peddling like BX Racers for the invisible line that marked the safe wrong side of the tracks.

In *The Absence of Angels*, I describe a scene where the kids are getting ready to ride the hell out of Dodge. One kid asks the (Indian) narrator, "Where's your bike?," and he replies, "I walked," and another kid says, "If he ever does again," and the Brown, Black, and Yellow kids ride off to leave him to face the losers named after Disney Ducks.

Fortunately, as red is the color of sunburn, not of people, he manages to face off with them because Disney Ducks aren't real clever and don't know the Real News of those they are trying to threaten.

Besides learning to run and ride and that the police were there to protect other people from you as well as to serve subpoenas and warrants, growing up in those neighborhoods taught me to suspect politically correct language. Avoiding "Beaner" when I am speaking of you or to you is an artificial load of crap, and the load is what people who secretly feel the truth of the epithet want everyone to focus on. Not the intention or the contextualized meaning of the word itself. You are a Bean in the cup of beans that germinate and generate.

Besides that, you really do love beans. "Chickpea" (besides "ah-voe-KAH-doe," which I taught you to say at sixteen months) was one of your first words. Red beans, black beans, garbanzos—you often eat your beans first and want more to be isolated from our salad and fed to you. One who loves beans is a beaner, though I shorten it to keep from offending the folks at Whole Foods to "Clara Bean."

So I hope by this book titled *Raising Bean* to suggest to you that we live in a circumlocutionary world of absurdity and bureaucratic worry that creates entanglement like Charles Dickens's Circumlocution Office in which everything is promised and nothing performed, in which people say what they don't mean and then do it to you.

Like Martin Luther King, I may not get there with you. But you will always be Clara Clearly Bean or Beaner.

Draining the Swamp

"Once upon a time," I say to Clara Bean, "there was a thing called Truth. Now this thing, which Human Beings ran across sometimes before it ran across them, was huge and wobbly and grew bigger when the Human Beings were not looking. They called it 'Bryozoa,' animal colonies that grew bit by bit by sticking together in a gelatinous ball, usually around water, which they called 'Life.'

"Time passed. Oodles of time, like the time of the stars and the figures outlined by them, testaments to the existence of Coyote and Frog and Buffalo Man and Woman (Buffalo Man had three stars in line hanging between the lines of his legs; Buffalo Woman's stars formed a triangle). Human Beings were happy in a contented sort of way. They understood Truth, and when they didn't, they could sit still for hours, thinking."

"What did they think about, Bumpa?"

"About how they were. About their stories that told them how they were and were to be for times to come."

"Sit-sitting?" Since birth, Clara Bean has said "sit-sit," an order to adults that was really a request. Sit-sit beside me? Play with me? Read to me? All contained in the "sit-sitting."

"Usually. But not always. Sometimes they thought these things as they went about being how they were."

You might wonder why she doesn't try to correct me, asking if I mean *who* they were. She's already learned that *how* a person is tells us exactly who that person is: a person who hunts well and brings meat and game back to his family is not merely a good hunter but also a man who enjoys providing for his family, and it is in the provision that he finds value and gratitude. A man who hunts and provides some meat but then wallows in self-pity, feeling that he isn't appreciated for being a hunter at all, good or bad or more likely neither good nor bad, who grumbles or moans, complains or whines, is a man who lives backward, thinking that it is about his getting something and not his giving that creates his value, and thus he will always feel insufficiently valued, ungrateful, and unhappy. Maybe you shouldn't bite the hand that feeds you, but the hand ought always to be happy in doing the feeding.

Bean knows these things because she's heard how a student of mine said she loves her boyfriend because he loves her. She's heard me go on like the north wind in winter telling her stories that say that love is given, not gotten; love is a gift like the one I freely give to her, a gift that gives to me because I love the act of loving her, not because she loves me.

"One day," I continue, "there was born to Buffalo Woman a little boy, Zoan, who decided that being called Zoan was denigrating and cruel and left him no choice but to pry himself loose from the gelatinous Truth of his mother's world. Buffalo Woman tried to teach him the teachings, and when Buffalo Man got home from work, as tired as he was from running away from strange new bearded creatures who appeared on the plains and in the valleys, he, too, tried to convince Zoan that being a part of the huge wobbly truth was better than being alone and having to discover all the truths from the time of the stars.

"'Here you may learn from your mother. From me. From your uncles and aunts, your grandmothers and grandfathers,' Buffalo Man said.

"Buffalo Woman agreed. While she knew just like Buffalo Man that the day would come when Zoan would become his own gelatinous part of the Truth and possibly move away to the other side of Bryozoa or even to another colony of Bryozoans on the far side of the river, she knew, too, that to do that Zoan needed to acquire the strength and wisdom that came from patience and thought and learning.

"Zoan was having none of it. 'I don't trust your Truth,' he said. 'Your Truth is the Old Truth. I feel like that's false.'

"'What's this "feel?"' his father thought. It was a new thing. 'But the Old Truth is the only Truth,' he said quietly.

"'Things change,' Zoan replied with all the smuggy tenor of youth.

'I was out gathering the other day and I ran into this guy who said we needed to experiment. He said we think too much. We need to feel more. I feel like he's right. I get tired of all this thinking all the time.'

"'What did this guy look like?' Buffalo Woman asked.

"'He was kind of gray. Soft and furry. Had a bushy tail.'

"The Buffalos exchanged looks. He nodded sagely. She winked knowingly. Both of them were thinking with a wink and a nod, 'Coyote.' What in Truth's name was Coyote doing in their neighborhood?

"'He have a name, this kind of gray guy with a bushy tail?'

"'I don't remember. Maybe Old Man? Something like that.'

"Buffalo Man nodded again. He didn't need to look at his wife to see her nod. He knew she knew.

"'He grin at you? He have teeth like nothing you've ever seen outside of the front grille of an Edsel?'

"'Yeah-uh,' Zoan said, his voice expressing suspicion. 'How did you know?'

"'Oh, honey,' Buffalo Woman said. 'That was only Coyote, Old Man. He was messing with you.'

"'How do you know?' Zoan demanded. 'You weren't there.'

"'She doesn't have to be there to see it,' Buffalo Man said. 'She knows the Truth. She knows Coyote will come around and get you to help him pick pine nuts or berries, saying if you do, he'll have too many and inevitably he'll drop several and they'll trickle down to you. The more labor you put in picking, the more that will trickle down.'

"'Meanwhile, Old Man will hang around Congress pushing papers first this way, then that way, and when you're all done, when all the pine nuts are picked and gathered, he'll tell you that you got your share of pine nuts by eating them while you picked.'

"Buffalo Man laughed, his horns shaking not at the Truth but in knowing the Truth. He got up and went over to Buffalo Woman to nudge her knowingly before asking if she needed help shucking the corn and she said, 'No, but a glass of wine would be nice,' so he went and poured out a full glass of white wine and set it beside her.

"Zoan, being young and full of feeling unchecked by awareness, gathered his things in a huff of hurt, stuffed them into his rucksack, and hurried toward the flap of the tent.

"'Hold on,' Buffalo Man said. 'Why don't you wait and have some food first? Then you can go see your new Old Man.'

"Zoan was sort of hungry. Come to think of it, he felt like he could eat a horse.

"They sat in silence, eating the corn tacos with pulled rabbit and a pine nut aioli. Buffalo Man poured out another glass of white wine for Buffalo Woman and a red blend for himself, offering a glass as a peace offering to Zoan who, with a show of reluctance, accepted.

"'So what else does Old Man say?' Buffalo Man asked, thinking it was time enough.

"Zoan thought, felt, did what Zoans do and said at last, 'He said he's going to drain the swamp.'

"Already seeing what would happen but unable to keep from speaking the Truth even to his own son, Buffalo Man said, 'Ask him this, okay? Ask him, "How is the swamp supposed to drain itself?"'

"'What's that mean?' Zoan demanded.

"'You remember a story about Coyote and the Mallard Duck girls?'

"'Ye-ah.'

"'Remember how Coyote goes across the river to be with them?'

"Zoan shook his head. 'No.'

"'He floats. On the surface.'

"'So?'

"Buffalo Woman said, 'If you float on the surface, you can't do anything. Not anything good, anyway, and you sure as heck aren't going to succeed in draining the swamp. On the surface, you may only add to the swamp. Increase it. Not decrease it.'

"'Floating on it, you're just going to be part of the swamp. You've got to dig a hole, dig down deep if you're going to drain it.'

"'He said that,' Zoan replied, all full of his righteousness. 'He said for me to bring a shovel next time I see him and we'll commence to digging.'

"'Be a pretty small hole,' Buffalo Woman said to herself. She didn't want to upset her son who was beginning to look all dried out, like a pine nut all alone on the ground.

"'One shovel, two diggers?' asked Buffalo Man. He knew. He knew that Old Man Coyote wasn't going to do much more than get up late and pretend to supervise the work that Zoan had to do. That was why he floated instead of swam. Old Man didn't expend any energy beyond figuring out how to trick people into doing what he thought he wanted done.

"'I'll be different,' Zoan said. 'Old Man says I won't be one of those who sit around doing nothing to make things better, but someone who is totally and completely very unique. Different. A patriot.'

"'So you need a shovel.' He did not remind Zoan that especially given where he came from, there was no such thing as 'very' unique. Indeed, unique itself, the concept, was suspect. People were people; the swamp was the swamp, and it was much like other swamps. If Old Man occupied the swamp, then how would he know what to drain, being all swampy himself? Would he drain out the water on which he floated? But Buffalo Man said nothing. Buffalo Man wanted to move away from arguing. His son would learn. Soon, he hoped, enough, but if not soon enough, maybe later in time.

"'As long as it's not too late,' he heard Buffalo Woman think. 'Indeed,' he thought in return, and they winked and nodded again, their horns doing a dance together.

"'Yep.'

"'There's one out back where I was digging up those fence posts the ranchers put in yesterday. Take it,' he said, already seeing his son prop the shovel on his shoulder and walk off into the dawn to wherever he expected to find Old Man and his swamp while also seeing, though less clearly, his son slip homeward some days hence practicing facial expressions, trying to look accomplished in the face of failure, trying to seem pleased on the surface while knowing all the while he was displeased, hoping his father and mother would not say, 'You see? We told you so.'

"The Buffalos both felt not sad, but wistful, wishing they could teach

Zoan enough to keep him from having to learn what he had to learn. Knowing they could not. And would not for that very reason: because he had to learn it. Otherwise it would all be surface and hair and the swamp goo twittering of greedy Myna birds as Zoan went about pretending to be different while being only the same but worse.

"And that is how it happened," I say to Clara Bean, wondering, What? What will happen how?

INTENTIONAL INDIANS

In the sixties, we turned from communal to personal, from meaning to superficial relevance, turning the whole of our grocery bill into the data of unit pricing. We believed that things could change if we only made people use the right words, dropping misnomers like "Indian" and replacing it with "American Indian" or "Native American." Self-righteous youth demanded that Stanford drop their mascot Indian. After Stanford's athletes began to play as the "Cardinals," they turned their virtue signaling against the then Cleveland Indians in a righteous attempt to rid the world of that team's cartoonish logo.

When things like pipelines began to gutter beneath sacred lands, or canyons and valleys were turned into suburban vistas, they became very, very angry and did things like organize and march. They held encounter sessions or set up annual Picnic Day celebrations with sheep herding and skimpy clothing that could lead to "free" love by day's end. They demanded that universities teach relevant courses like human sexuality, as long as the professor in front of the largest and most well-attended lecture at UC Davis did not mention STDs except by implication when he explained the use of condoms. He claimed that the male penis was one of the cleanest parts of a human body and therefore we ought to wash our hands before urinating, not after, which only proves to me that said professor was not, and had never imagined being, an old man dribbling his way toward incontinent death. We did not like the discomforts of truth.

If they were going to stop calling ships "she," then they had little choice but to switch to calling Black people "Black" (afterward changed to "African American" or the circular "people of color" which means—literally—"colored people" and only identifies its user as a person who likes extra unnecessary words in their bureaucratic thinking). As for life itself, well, there's the example of one's student Zoë, who doesn't want to be referred to as "she." The problem is that life doesn't eff her over any more than she effs over herself, and in fact, her "life" is just that, life—which is truly a miracle even when it isn't going well.

They also thought we needed to drop "Native American" and put in something else, given the absence of "American" when Natives began to trip-trap over the troll bridge to Alaska and down to the lower forty-eight, and "well-tanned person from a large swath of the Americas" (once Amerigo Vespucci got to sailing around and lending his forename to continents connected by the isthmatic esophagus of "central" America) wasn't imprecise enough.

One might adopt the method of naming Indians by their original tribe, despite the fact that many of the original tribes have since mixed their so-called blood when they met and married people from other tribal persons removed from their ancestral lands to boarding schools and reserves, as were the Osage and Nez Perce. Of course, the Osage weren't just removed—Whites often married and then murdered them in order for a White husband to get his hands on the oil leases owned by each Osage after vast repositories of the fossil goo were discovered beneath the barren, untenable lands set aside by the federal government for the Osage to rebuild their villages and communities on. And the Nez Perce, who did not want to fight, had first to be captured by the unbelievably inept US Cavalry as they walked—walked—north, pausing to rest a mere thirty miles from the Canadian border, to their endless regret. Had they only kept going they'd now be able to be First Nations and First Peoples in a civilized country of people who end every sentence, "Eh?" ("Ā")?

Had the cavalry given the Nez Perce another day or two, they'd not have had to deal with them at all, but it seemed so much more fun to attack and kill. Besides, the cavalry were so embarrassed by their ineptitude that they were kind of pissy, angry, even furious. It *seemed* more fun to kill the Indians. But they first had to deal with Nez Perce sharpshooters—among the best of the century—which is almost a genetic impulse that I have demonstrated by moving right or left quickly or jumping up and down as though on horseback and still hitting the bull's eye in the backyard with a bow and arrow or a BB rifle. I've done it as well on a firing range in ROTC, though the surprise and admiration of the supervising army lieutenant was more dimmed than my backyard barbecue friends.

So we could call the Osage "Osage" and Nez Perce "Nez Perce" and suffer the indignities of the politically correct correcting us Nez Perce with "Nay Pur-say" because it was a misnomer applied to three pierced nose warriors come across by French trappers beavering deep into the Wallowa Valley to whom we snidely reply, "Really, it's Nu-mi-pu or, in the instance of Osage, Wazhzáhe, you drip."

Perhaps that was what Chief Joseph really was saying when the romanticizing, self-justifying White folks wrote down his "I will fight no more forever" monologue? Was he really saying—calmly, because to get upset or run around pissing on the campfires is undignified in a way that some White folks on the internet don't seem to understand as they bare their bottoms both metaphorically and actually online— "You bloody drips are the angriest murderers I've ever seen and fighting with you is of no use to me given that I am thirty men, women, and children, and you are hundreds fresh from lynching and burning some innocent poor Black youth for writing a note to a White woman," or maybe, "A trip to Leavenworth may be like a trip to Disneyland, eh?" Without the rides, of course.

One thing we know is that once Joseph surrendered, he surrendered. He didn't sit around plotting to pay the White folks back for their chasing his band all the way to almost Canada. Though they understand the idea less and less, he had given his word, and his word was, as it was to Beowulf, his "wyrd," his fate and his final future. Was he happy about it? No. Was it the way he had envisioned his retirement from chief of tribe or leader of band? No. And envisioning the near and distant future is a part of Nez Perce being.

Story—not legend or history, but story, which is true—has it that Joseph, Hinmot Tooyoolakhtet, spent a good deal of his time roaming Leavenworth and its pristine, barren environs talking, speaking to himself and to his fathers and grandfathers, mothers and grand-mothers, with maybe an aunt or uncle tossed in for good measure along with a prairie dog or two. This is an activity I recognize because I, too, talk with my grandfather, all the more when department politics rear their gorgonic head and people who have never published much of importance if at all argue that their merit raises ought to equal the merit raises of people who have published a good deal. Being Native, Black, male, female, or gay does not make up for an absence, a blank-ness on the line of the curriculum vita where publications should be noted in bibliographical form (MLA style).

I am even more active in talking to Grandfather when I have messed up—when I've unintentionally hurt someone else's feelings or behaved in a way that is unbefitting a Human Being, and the last time I spoke with Grandfather, he said that yes, I did mess up and I ought to seek out the person and apologize.

At other times, he has reminded me of the problems with "intention."

Now, in 1946, two scholars named W. K. Wimsatt and Mon-roe Beardsley published an essay titled "The Intentional Fallacy," which opened an entire case of canned fish for me, leaking an oily stink out over my intention to become a scholar and critic as well as a writer of other things unread. "The Intentional Fallacy" became a touchstone.

Everyone, Bean, has touchstones, things, people, or events that have such an effect on one's being that they get remembered always. Often-times, these people arrive in the shifting shapes of teachers—Miss White, Marion MacNamara, George P. Elliott, Donald Dyke, Jack Hicks, and Arthur Amos—or in the shape of publishers—Permanent Press and Judy Shepard or *Southern Humanities Review*—or friends like Eric Boyer, or Susan and Peter Valenti—or writer friends like Ray-mond Carver—or the characters one meets in books, like the Buendías in *One Hundred Years of Solitude* or Tom Crick in *Waterland* or Portia in Elizabeth Bowen's great *The Death of the Heart* or the inimi-table Beowulf or Odysseus, the master storyteller himself.

Other times they come in experiences like the Uffizi in Florence, Notre Dame in Paris, the endless Bruegel paintings in Belgium, the

National and National Portrait Galleries in London, the Courtauld Institute, the Barnes Collection in Philly, or the Shetland Islands, Kiel Canal, Dublin, and Glendalough just south of it, and if nothing else, one realizes as the list grows and goes how fortunate one has been to be alive. To have lived engaged with reading and viewing and thinking. There is a Matisse painting in Copenhagen that will always hang like a transparent screen through which I see the world, and of course there is his Chapelle du Rosaire de Vence in southern France. Lordy, lucky. Someday I might even manage a hole-in-one at the game old men play, golf, though it's looking less and less likely. Ah, well, eh?

Wimsatt, or maybe it was Beardsley, obviously spent his time engaged with nothing more than getting, and the getting was tenure at whatever university he taught at (even the word "taught" creates problems for me, since he probably did not teach but lectured on plot or agenda with a certainty that allowed the weaker-minded students in front of him to believe like parishioners).

Was it Beardsley or Wimsatt who decided that not being writers themselves they could cut out the middleman and go straight to the falsehood? And what they cut out is the editor, the writer who revises, or the professional reader who makes a writer, as some claim Gordon Lish made Ray Carver or Albert Erskine, Faulkner. As you, reader, make me.

They cut out editing agents like Alice Speilburg, and they cut out the Philip Booth who ran into Wallace Stevens at a writer's colony and said he'd worked all morning to get one good stanza, to which Stevens replied with exclamation that he'd work all day to get one good line. An amusing anecdote, perhaps, but one that contains a truth neither scholar ever encountered—and would not, even if that truth were a bus that ran them both over on a hot and humid morning uptown.

A writer's job is to pay attention to the effect his words have on his audience. If that effect is not achieved when he rereads his work, then he has to change it, edit it, modify it so that it gets as close as he is able to get it before publication.

If that is true, then whenever he publishes it, his intention is plain. It's in the words, the structure for the process of reading, for the revelation of character, the kind of language they speak or think in. It's in the metaphors and similes, and descriptions, the contexts in which the book happens (and "rehappens"). If they are right, the intelligent, sensitive, well-read reader recognizes and enjoys them all, and pretty much in the way the author intended. In regard to "intention," then, there are only two things that may be said: a writer either succeeded or failed to match his intentions with his resulting manuscript. There is no fallacy that the reader engages in except for the fallacy of the person who thinks he knows when he doesn't—like many of my students in the early days of a semester.

In other words, if the sensitive, intelligent, linguistically aware reader cannot discern and determine a writer's intention, then the writer has failed to place his words in the proper order. Consider a poem by Emily Dickinson with the line "burglar, banker, father." Professor Charles X—whose last name, along with his importance to my overall education, escapes me—wanted to invert the word order to mean what he wanted it to mean and, when I—a presumptuous dick of a graduate student—insisted that you could not alter the word order in order to screw out a particular meaning, he replied that I was wrong. Fortunately for him, and for me, it was early in the semester and I could drop the class by asking George P. Elliott to supervise an independent study in nineteenth-century American poetry (see above list), which he did, happily telling me privately and secretly that I should avoid classes from Professor X, about which George need not have worried (oh, dang, I just remembered X's last name and with his name comes the square and untested facial expression, which will haunt the rest of my day).

When Heinrich Böll titles a story "The Thrower Away," you must understand why being a thrower away makes the narrator with his three advanced degrees feel alienated and why he's a problem for a commercial society—although you may also understand that your students, who are only twenty and, being American, have the philosophical apparatuses of twelve-year-olds, have not yet risen to their rest and fallen into a fountain's bowl of understanding. They yet need to discard agendas in order to achieve some peace and simplicity, some clarity in which their time is not wasted by all the brochures we have to open and discard—brochures that arrive daily in classrooms or through the mail and now with that beneficial horror called the internet on email. Seriously, how many times is Sirius XM radio going to solicit me with yet another brochure or emailed warning that I am about to miss out on subscribing to a service that I will never use? I have already received at least a hundred, even after a telephone call that I answered in an effort to be courteous, to tell them siriusly that I was uninterested and would remain uninterested in subscribing to their service. Now I throw away mailings from them unopened, and (thank God for caller ID) I do not take their calls, and periodically I empty the trash bin replete with their unopened emails.

To be fair, I never open unwanted or unrecognized emails, and I rarely take any phone calls. Period. Except from family, and friends of whom I have fortunately few.

I work at home at work that brooks little interruption. Thus the ringer—land line and cell—is usually turned off because there is nothing more painful than holding in your mind a wonderful sentence (that may have to be edited out) only to have the phone ring and the syllables scatter like roaches to their respective holes and corners.

What about outside of writing? Bean may ask. What about the Stanford or Cleveland Indians and their mascot logos that could, to some or many, seem insulting or denigrating?

What do they have to do with me? I'd reply.

You're Nez Perce.

Yep. So?

An Indian mascot often makes Indians look sort of silly and stupid.

The once Cleveland Indians' mascot made people think only of the baseball team, not Cleveland, not Ohio, and definitely not Indian. The mascot has a feather, sure, but it's pointing straight up like a middle finger at someone or something; it's not like a feather tucked into the back of your hair to indicate having counted coups—which might be touching an opponent with a stick or blunt end of a spear as much as shooting him with a bullet or arrow. So what does that silly cartoon have to do with a Nez Perce—Osage Bumpa? Its intentional object is not me and even the common use of romanticized Indians in white folk lore seems a bit of a stretch, don't you think? Sure, campus Indians who want to play Indian in order to protect their tenure and puff up their merit for monetary increase may take offense. But at what do they not take offense? One, I know, even accused me of unfavorably reviewing his first (and only) novel for his eventual publisher, which was a lie cooked up by his maybe Indian friend who wanted to remain the director of Indianness on campus and not have to compete with anyone. There was no way—if he'd thought about it, if he were capable of thinking clearly—that he could have known how I reviewed his novel, given the strict confidentiality of the process. My only regret, having reviewed it favorably, is that I did say to publish it. I did it because he was a colleague new to me whom others said they wanted to keep, even though the novel itself truly sucked. So I sold a piece of my soul for a piece of nothing, and that seems to be not intentional but deserved. And kind of funny.

"Have you told him?"

"I've thought about it."

"And?"

"What's the use? What would be my intentions all these years later? To make him feel bad? He wouldn't believe me. Besides, if I were he, I'd feel bad enough just being he."

"So what should I do when Mrs. Weary asks me how I feel about the Indians? She's a big fan."

"Well," I say, thinking. "I guess keep to yourself. Learn from the teachers who teach and ignore the ones who preach. Consider your home, and Bumpa's home as well, your own reserve, and watch your immigration laws."

THE SIXTIES

"What was it like in the sixties, Bumpa?"

Clara has called me "Bumpa" since the day she bumped her infant head on the low side of a table and I asked, "You bump your head?," patting my noggin with an open palm. Since then, her mother told me, she'd often wake from her nap, pat her head, and ask, "Bumpa?" inquiring, the way infants may, if Grandpa was coming to her house. When she got in the van to come to our house—which was six days a week on average—she recognized the way and began patting her head again with "Bumpa?" Had she more than patted, I'd have worried about early onset concussions and the assured dementia that came from repeated head banging. But she, like her mom, is the gentlest of happy souls. With the good fortune that has plagued my life, she now lives next door, and many are the mornings when drinking tea I watch her run out to her play structure, back to the house to get a hoodie against the fall's chill air, and then back out to swing and spin on her belly talking to herself all the while. Yesterday I was struck by seeing her walk, waving her hands, and talking—to herself, to the birds, to the trees and flowers and bushes. That's the other thing that Clara does. Talk. Even when she's chewing gum.

This month, Clara is doing a family history project for Mrs. Weary, her underpaid and overworked teacher. Weary is twenty-seven, with a twenty-something's eager enthusiasm and hopefulness and has yet to have her energy mined by the insidious "programs" and slogans Education Departments and school administrators annually invent in order to keep their mysteries current. Education Departments are like a coven of witches who alter the sounds and sights and symbols of their ritual of sacrificing the brains of victims in order to retain their tendential influence over the way children are sliced and diced and turned into the stews of entitled failure. I liked Mrs. Weary from the very first because of the human way she said to call her Antanina, smiled, and said, "So you're Bumpa."

Guilty.

Liking Antanina as much as Clara seemed to, I wanted to help make her project a good one. Clara would choose from any and all of my stories about the sixties—and believe me, I have a few. The seventies, too, and the eighties. But those would take their rightful place in the later grades. If and when they became acceptable, if not appropriate. If riding freight trains up and down the western states ever would be appropriate for a child to hear. A lot of teachers, with the currency of educationist jargonizing, skipped history altogether or altered it, in that cute little way educationists have, to "herstory," and then complained about how men had dominated history. That ignored the fact of Margaret Thatcher and Nancy Dominatrix Reagan, Cleopatra and Mata Hari and Catherine the Great, or Barbara Bush, not to mention the queen of England, Elizabeth, who at this moment is into her beloved nineties. But that's all ancient history.

"The sixties?" I said, then "hmmm," using the age-old technique of buying time while seeming to consider and think—something that can get just a wee bit difficult when you're older and just adding up your golf score is a challenge. "Well," I said slowly, "we thought the sixties were different, a change from all that had come before, and not an expected transition from *Leave It to Beaver* to bell-bottomed pants and the Nehru jackets of the seventies."

"Doesn't Secretary of State Clinton wear bell-bottoms and Nehru jackets?" Clara asked. "After all, you were the one who said . . ."

"So the sixties were turbulent," I said, not wanting to hear whatever I might have said about the Clintons. George W. might be fair game. But not Hillary. I probably made a joke about her seeming inauthenticity and the way she appears stunned and smiling when she gives a fireside chat or speech, where she could hide most of her flare behind a widened podium. My jokes often are in poor taste, and though I frequently describe myself in negative terms of appearance, I understand how it can hurt if someone else describes me the same way—like my wife, who calls me her "cheese curd," hinting broadly that I might have donned a few pounds too many.

"Tur-byoo what?"

"Turbulent," I said, trying to enunciate each syllable. "They were a decade of protest. Marches. Really they were a lot of draft-aged children who wanted to protest being sent against their will to a jungle called Vietnam."

"Like you?"

"Like me. A whole lot of people my age joined together to raise social consciousness. Blacks, Whites, Reds, Browns, and Asians," I said, hoping she didn't notice how I changed color for geography. "Yellow" seemed, well, so yellow. So inaccurate.

"While we were at it, we subdivided: Blacks had their reasons to protest, and they called it 'Black Power' and raised their fists and bowed their heads on the medals podium at the Olympics; Latinos created unions and marched to ask for fairer wages and less harsh conditions for farmworkers. They mainly wanted biplanes to quit swooping down along the furrows of shimmering hot fields to spray the fields and them with pesticides. But they also asked to have new shacks to cram their families into when they ate and slept, which, fortunately, the farm owners did not allow much of. White and part-White kids joined both groups—not at the Olympics, of course, being overfed losers ourselves—and protested being middle class and privileged. We felt like we were making a difference while at the same time proving to the country that we were not what the country thought."

"Mommy said you weren't privileged."

"I wasn't exactly White either. I was poor, but the house I lived in growing up was on the outside edge of the neighborhood; we were not as poor as the Blacks whose houses backed up to the railway lines. Not as poor as people who stooped and bent and picked all day in the hot sun so they could earn enough to drive their beat-up pickups back to Chiapas and live out the winter months eating beans." I paused and took a moment to remember my school girlfriend, Margaret Rocha,

with whom, with a flashlight in a closet, I'd explored the visual difference between boys and girls. Her parents owned a small restaurant
and her sister died from lead poisoning not because some Republicans
decided utility surmounted humanity in Flint, Michigan, but because
the hazing to join a Mexican sorority was drinking a certain amount of
leaded gasoline. The more you drank, the higher your initial ranking
in the club, and Rita wanted to start at the top, not work her way up.

"Bumpa?"

"Yes. Sorry." When you get old, the memories crowd together
like wraiths around a vat of blood.

Aha! Maybe that was it. The sixties were a decade when privilege
was relative but real. A decade when every Tom, Dick, and Jamayl
weren't entitled to whatever without achieving any of it. When POCs
(by which I mean not people of color, but people of cracker) didn't fall
for the con of lower tax rates that would save them $150 a year while
saving the bill's proponent somewhere in the millions.

"At least there was such a relative thing," I added. "Not an absolute
with 'Us' and 'Them.' Like now." Oh, well. "So what are we doing?"

Clara had white poster board laid out on the coffee table, her box
of markers and pens neatly arranged around it. She drew a pencil line
across the top. Above it, she printed "ThE SiXtiEs" in red. Then she
put a numeral 1 in the margin, and I helped her spell "Turbulent."
Below that she began printing words like "Black." Though I assumed
Antanina Weary would refer to Blacks as "African Americans," I
just couldn't. Growing up in the fifties and asked by Negroes in the
sixties to call them "Blacks," the word was too ingrained now to
change the terminology yet again. I didn't see how changing the
terms changed the continuous racism that continues to be perpetrated
against Black people. I have little truck with terminologies, anyway.
After all, a base Republican could use the words "African Americans" and still from the disgusted sound of his voice let you know
he meant "niggers." In an opposite way, Joseph Conrad's wonderful
novella *The Nigger of the Narcissus* could no longer be taught, even

though James Wait, the "nigger," was the binding force and soul of the ship *Narcissus*. The pearl in the center of the shipboard oyster.

Just because someone did or did not call you "a dick" did not ameliorate the fact that you still acted like one as Stormy Daniels chased you about the swank hotel room spanking your tighty-whities with a rolled-up *Forbes* with a satirical picture of you on the front (though not colluding with satire, you don't realize that).

Changing what one calls a group of people was no proof that the endemic racism of America had diminished. Not only did real estate agents steer Black clients toward homes in neighborhoods no one other than Black, Brown, or Red people lived in, but also banks found excuses not to give mortgages to the most deserving of Black couples. Heaven help you if the couple seeking a loan from the bank was biracial. But even the insult that would result from that was better than being strangled by police because you were big or being shot dead for running away or worse, for being a Black twelve-year-old carrying an unconcealed toy pistol, an insult that allowed the good people to comment on how things were getting better for Blacks while it still made the "good" people wearing Klan hoods angry. Back when Stokely Carmichael asked us to call him Black, I was liberal; now I realized that if I were Black I think I'd buy an NRA automatic rifle and begin shooting White folks out of frustration and fury.

Still, the generation I now teach—X-ers or Z-ers or iGen—is one of the least dismissive or apparently racist I've seen. They are accepting. They are so accepting that they simply laugh at politicians' continuous lies as though things don't matter like Supreme Courts or voting rights. It's a cynical laughter that worries me, and cynicism is a wearing and wearying disease.

"Bumpa?"

"Oh. Sorry. How about 'Collaborative'?"

"Colab what?"

"Groups. Young people banding together to tell people how to think the right way."

"What if it wasn't?"

"No 'if' about it. Ifs were not allowed. Ifs were banned. First from speech. Then from thought."

"So is that number three?"

Where'd two go? It's amazing how the older you get, the more things run together into meaningless opacities like old people in rest homes drooling on about things that matter only to them, if they do. I mean they immigrated to these shores, distributed smallpox-infested blankets or shot down Native women and children while they stole the land, and now they want to Make America Gag Again by keeping the land for the people who belong here? Ever looked into the Osage murders? And we, Native or former immigrant, expect things to be different?

"How about some blue? Here. You see, if you draw a wavy red line down the page, then you can color one side black and the other blue."

"Okay." Bean pulled out her black and blue markers and uncapped them both after drawing a long wavy line down the poster. She's good at wavy lines, as though she intuits the fact that causality is only a wavy line ironed straight, like Black girls' hair before the afro said everything it needed to.

When she was finished, having colored her blacks and blues ever larger as though some internal artistic sense refused to be satisfied until nearly the entire center of the poster was black and blue divided by red, she handed the markers to me to cap. She stood back, appraising her work, and said, "It's kinda ugly."

"I think it's fine," I said. Weary of thinking about the sixties.

"There's not much to it," she said, neither condemning her work nor praising it.

"That's the sixties," I said.

2

RACE AND IDENTITY

I Stand Here Listening

Bean comes to me disturbed, distressed, dismayed. I can tell. The humanity of her feelings comes from her parents who have kept her from the addictions of youth like video games, movies (unless they're ballets of *The Nutcracker* or *Don Quixote*), and the handheld tools for narcissistic masturbation called cellular phones. Before she was two years old she could say "ah-voe-KAH-doe" properly, although *Nutcracker* came out "Nut-sacker," and she began to tell funny jokes that none of us understood, looking around at our faces and laughing, pleased that we, too, were laughing, though with love and not at the punchless punch line.

By three, she understood far more than a three-year-old ought to, causing us all to be extra careful in what we said, though I have to admit that generally our language and subject were calm and reflective, until a game-show host got elected president, and we were daily faced with his disgusting self-love, his curiously perverse relations with his daughter, and his two sons with plastic doll's hair. Then the things we said often ramped up beyond the acceptable.

I understood why some less-than-logical people would vote for a person as different as he seemed; I teach at a university where political correctness and liberal agenda have overreached their limits with their need until I have heard more than one administrator say, "I am not going to deny tenure to a woman, especially not a minority woman," and I've heard the subject of that statement protest and claim that blogs—unvetted, unreviewed dribblings of a neurotic mind—should count as "publication" for merit raises and promotion. I have been to meetings where, were I to say what I really think, I'd be shouted down and forced to live out my life in solitary rejection instead of the solitary introverted self-repression I accept as my state.

It is this necessary self-repression that foresightless voters thought they voted out as they voted in the very people who ensured that Washington did not work for the citizenry. Forty-six of the 47 percent of people who voted for Old Feckless voted against their own self-interests and not in an altruistic way. They were slated to be hurt economically and socially; the other "1 percent" made something like $247 billion in one calendar year. Not too much stress, I hope, paying the mortgage on the five or six mansions and the upkeep on their airplanes. But the Lower 46 were tired of the overextension of what got tagged as "liberalism," which to my thinking is good, but which, when overextended, becomes a kind of antiliberal repression.

Not wanting Beaner to feel repressed, not by Bumpa at least, I ask her what's wrong. After all, she is alternately frowning and smiling, thinking about something and yet pleased to be with Bumpa, and God knows I don't want her cheeks to begin hanging with the bulldog jowls of women before they go in for Botox or surgery, thinking that having the tight facial skin of a twelve-year-old perched on the neck of a lizard is going, somehow, to reverse the effects not only of time but also of character. Not to mention attitude.

"So what's up?" I ask.

"DeVon got expelled from school." DeVon, during those wonderful ages when neither gender's rain, nor the sleet of race, nor the wintry mix of gods or prophets keeps kids from their appointed play, is her best friend.

"Ah. That's serious," I add, buying time to wonder if DeVon did something like touch her inappropriately or hit her in the face, for either of which he might be expelled from the joys of schooling, less to do him good than in recognition of the putrid educationist's pungent rubrics and complete lack—"zero"—of tolerance for kids being kids. Afraid of the answer, I ask her what he did and she replies, "He threw a snowball at me."

"Oh my god," I blurt.

"Is that bad?"

"Very," I reply, thinking that in Illinois he could have been killed for that. Shot down by police who claim he had a hand grenade. Maybe tackled and strangled like Eric Garner.

I could hear the battalions of mankind standing stolidly by and trying to explain that were DeVon's snowball to hit Beaner in the face, it might make her uncomfortable for long enough to laugh or giggle or rush off to make a snowball to throw back at him, two kids having fun and taking pleasure in each other's spirited company and grammar school affection. But the battalions are more concerned with danger: a snowball might blind her or, worse, injure her self-esteem because DeVon's snowballs are bigger, rounder, more firmly packed, and therefore harder than hers, a microaggression that boys pack bigger and throw better.

It's bad when the pertinent intellectual question "So effing what?" has been replaced by meaningless phrases called microaggressions.

People who use terms like "microaggressions" seem to me to be people who want to control the world with totalitarian self-righteousness, and they want to change the words in order to effect that control.

But first of all, they can't. They may not control the world by changing the words. In the infamous sixties, in college, I complained bitterly that making "she" ships into "he or she" ships accomplished little more than to allow a fundamentally sexist (girl or boy) to remain fundamental. Changing the language had no effect on the response except to slow things down, avoid the naming of parts. The remainder—enfranchisement, equal pay for equal work, mutual respect, Title IX—was merely logical and just. The rest was using words to, well, *utilize* words, reaffirming the poisonous gases of bureaucracy, passivity, and confoundable meaning while expanding the periodic table with the illusions of choice.

Asserting moral authority, a haughty conceit.

Even Hester Prynne with her scarlet letter probably went around thinking thoughts you'd describe as "ill" and wondering if maybe Mordechai Tilman might not want to dillydally out beyond the village among the root and squirrel of the forest. And I have no doubt but that the most morally outraged of Hester's neighbors were the women and men who had hanky-panky in their hearts and minds. Their Bible tells them that only those free from sin may cast the first stone, and yet they go around not only casting stones but also trying to inscribe in stone rules of behavior that would keep their neighbors from enjoying what they themselves may desire.

DeVon is not a sex offender; he is a little boy. Perhaps an overly inquisitive little boy, but then that's boyhood. Even if he touched Bean on the buttocks—which at her age lack all tocks—the correction of that behavior is not up to rules and schools but up to parents—and guess what, most kids' parents, though physically present, are absent, too concerned with getting and spending to think.

Actually, many of them don't think—they react—and parents, even the ones who did not vote populist (racist), are incapable of thought, of philosophy, of laughing at their own insignificance. In their reactions they reveal their lack of philosophy and humor and prove their willingness to invest in scarlet letters and rules in stone made for other people. Were they thoughtful people, DeVon's parents would teach him that maybe sometimes another kid might not want to be touched in just those ways. But, oh, I forgot, DeVon's parents are too busy satisfying their own small needs and desires, and so (rather insistently) have turned over their roles and responsibilities to some poor schmuck who is underpaid and overworked and who went into teaching with all sorts of curious hopes and expectations such as they might actually be allowed to teach the little effers to read about something, to understand nuance and context for things, gain empathy through literature and reflective understanding through history and philosophy, and not worry over ridiculous standardized tests made up by fools in Education Departments because if the little effers don't do well enough on the tests, the poor schmuck's absurdly low salary won't ever rise, and, believe me, the job is a very difficult time- and energy-consuming one that may not be coal mining but, except for the dust and black lung, might as well be. Come to think of it, is there a black brain disease? A

cancer of the mind that allows any man to have orange hair and actually admit that he does not read? Am I taking crazy pills?

But I don't say all this to Beaner. In fact, I don't say any of this, but
with great effort, grabbing my right hand with my left to keep from
banging myself on the forehead, I do what any sensible adult would
do and ask, "For throwing a snowball. At you."

"Yes."

"For . . ." I am rendered speechless. I'm already chewing my lower
lip like it's gum.

"It was my fault," Bean says, almost a whisper. "I threw one at him,
first. Mrs. Woofer didn't see me. When he went and rolled a bigger ball
and threw it at me, she ran over, grabbed DeVon, and hauled him off
to the warden." We call the principal "the warden" out of principle. As
a lad, I spent hours with the princi-*pals* of my grammar schools.

"Did you tell her?"

"Yes." This, I realize, is what was bothering her, why her voice is con-
gested with the pneumonia of regret and worry. This is her confession,
and her plea. She's asking what to do.

"And?"

"Mrs. Woofer said that he could have hurt me. That he might have
poked my eye out or worse, caused me to fall from the climbing structure onto the padded, rubberized surface below."

"But you told her that you threw a snowball first."

"I said. Yes."

"What did Woofer woof?"

"She ignored me. She said it was not right that a schools-of-
choice boy should be allowed to try to hurt one of the students who
belonged here."

"Ah." What she said was that there were good people on both sides
of Charlottesville, some wearing hoods and swastikas and carrying
tiki torches and shouting racial slurs or "Jews will not replace us," the
others chanting "Give peace a chance" and handing out bouquets of
paper flowers. What she said is that Black boys like DeVon should stay

where they belong, on the far side of town and not make her spend her tax dollars busing him over to a school in which he has half a chance of getting an education—the same half a chance that any middle-class kid has in this world of education in which standards have died. What she said is that a Black boy who doesn't want to be taken down in a hail of police gunfire should keep his blooming snowballs to himself.

Gritting my teeth, the only response these days to insanity, I asked, "And she thinks DeVon does not belong at your school?"

Bean frowns. The question is clear to her. So is the answer. I can hear, in my listening, that, and I am proud.

To Have and On Hold

The spirit of liberty is the spirit which is not too sure that it is right.

Judge Learned Hand

I t's winter. Sleet one week, hurricanes the next, followed by a hot spell emigrating from Africa in a caravan of climate denial. This afternoon it's freezing rain as the mothers and I await the offspring outside the fortified entrance to the elementary school. When we speak it's like whales clearing their blowholes, streams and clouds of steam forming before rapidly dissipating. I am the only male and this is the Midwest where even men known to be retired from the getting and spending of the workaday world are viewed with suspicion. As there is always a part of me that I hold apart, separate from groups of people agreeing with themselves, quietly nodding when called upon, these mothers have come to accept if not like me.

"Where's Clara's mom?" Mrs. Macon puffs. Medium height, behind wire-rimmed spectacles beneath a helmet of tight curls, Mrs. Macon teaches at the local college.

"Working," I reply. I don't elaborate.

Mrs. Arleigh aims her spear of steam at me. "You actually let your daughter get a job?" She knows me. Or she believes she does. Expensively attired with a strand of real pearls beneath her tailored wool coat, she thinks she's the prettiest mom in the school. She doesn't like me. "Where?"

"The city."

"The city. As in our city?"

I nod. She worked two years for our city and was so able and efficient that when she quit to stay at home they asked her to work one afternoon a month to keep her registered on the city's payroll, hoping that when Clara was old enough she'd return to work for them. She won't. She prefers the atmosphere of severely controlled budgeting and the continuous and tiring process of stay-at-home momdom to the acquisition of money, power, or things. About not working outside the home, she's adamant.

"You think women should stay at home," Mrs. Arleigh steams.

"No, I don't." What I think is that everyone has to work it out for herself.

I often wonder at Mrs. Arleigh. She comes to parent meetings towing her husband, Todd, a subservient male of the species who agrees with everything she says. He's not a bad guy if you get him alone, though he is a tad boring. In fact, I've come to call being dull being "a tad Todd."

Like many of the other men in the room, Todd "works," by which we mean he gets up every weekday morning and trudges off to an office where he occupies space behind a desk or dons a yellow hard hat and safety glasses while supervising a warehouse or a manufacturing operation in times when America had factories that made things that needed storage in warehouses, long before these factories became empty expanses of weed-infested asphalt behind high chain-link fences with plywood panels hiding the openings that once were windows.

His work, no doubt, conditions him. At least, his having to be around coworkers and to get along with them, using language like they use in the way that they use language, modifies his perceptions. Todd might well be a lawyer, or a government official justifying the high levels of lead in Flint's drinking water.

Mrs. Arleigh feels anger and resentment at what she assumes is her husband's happiness in the world of work outside the home. She is caught having to stay at home minding the kids, taking care of the house (a very nice house, ranch-style, with a driveway that curves in front of a three-car garage that contains two expensive cars and a riding mower that converts into a snowplow). Todd vacuums for her, and yet Mrs. Arleigh says he's crap at vacuuming. She makes jokes out of his talent for cooking one particular dinner dish, tuna quesadillas. Her jokes are bitter, underscoring her resentment at having to pick up the kids from soccer as well as the household slack. The "stay at homeness" of it all. And not without reason: in a country where a person's value is measured by money, by what you "have" and not by how you "do," such resentment seems completely reasonable.

If I were a woman, it would be the expectation that I'd do these chores that would grate. If it's worked out, an agreement not unlike Mrs. Macon's with her husband, then it's fair. It's a choice. One that is made and one that may be altered at some point in the future.

A person who stays home with the house and kids works double if not triple time, and the work is stultifying. "Really? You want me to read you *Goodnight Moon* for the four hundred and fortieth time?" (*Goodnight Moon* is one of the good ones. Imagine trying to act curious, again, like Curious George).

Choices are hard to remember and to live by. They are also sometimes hard to recognize. The Nez Perce know that how you live up to point A may not only create the opportunity to make a certain choice, it also might well seem to predetermine how you will make the choice. So a Nez Perce like Grandfather spent a good amount of time meditatively thinking, not merely understanding how he got to be how he was but how to pass that "how" on to his grandchildren, to give them not the freedom to be how they liked but the spirit of liberty, and as Judge Learned Hand famously said, "The spirit of liberty is the spirit which is not too sure that it is right."

It is in this spirit that previously I have seemed to agree with the general statements and tenor of Mrs. Arleigh, or one of the other moms, like Mrs. Macon or Mrs. Heather. Mrs. Heather is a solid, gentle soul who reads books and often takes a line that is conflicting to Mrs. Macon's. Mrs. Macon also reads books, but books she may use in her education classes, though "use" for Mrs. Macon gets transformed into "utilize," believing the utility of "utilize" is to make the user seem more intelligent, although writers like William Kennedy might disagree.

Both women are likable, as long as you do not cross Mrs. Macon's red line and question whether feminism should not give women the right to choose to work or not to work for money. Arguing with Mrs. Macon has been a pleasure for me. What other pleasure is there when you're standing around outside the school waiting for the bell of liberty to ring and school to end and you don't want or need to listen to Mrs. Arleigh berate her tad Todd?

So I have nodded and smiled in apparent agreement with many of the easy nearly formulaic attitudes that get kicked around like hacky sacks. And it is in this nodding and smiling that I feel a little bit dirty, a little bit dishonest, and a lot lazy, unwilling to try, as I wait for Bean, to explain what it is I really think about women's right to work.

Leaving aside my historical issues with the word "right," which often needs to be rephrased as "wish" or "want"—I don't really believe in human rights, but I do strongly believe that we ought to want human beings to live the fullest, safest, most meditative and peaceful lives they can and that we ought to do whatever we may to forward the processes that lead in that direction.

Regarding work, of course a woman ought to have the right to work for equal pay; the equal should be to rank and not to gender. Plenty of Native women have led their band, their people. Plenty of them have guided with authority and wisdom and foresight, and though I tend toward a preference for women by thinking that women often exhibit more in the way of wisdom than a lot of men, that might be the result of men's having dominated the larger, non-Native "culture" for centuries, and thus it is men who have accumulated a long, broad history of ineptitude and unwisdom. We might also offer the idea that it's not just men but wealthy men, men who replace their human desire to do well and good, or to do good well, with a desire to acquire. What they want to acquire almost doesn't matter. Usually, of course, they think it is money or land and things that represent money or land, like slaves or Melanial concubines, women who will ignore what their husbands are grabbing that is not land or money. And yet nothing, from my point of view, is—acquired, that is.

Take land. You might say (and have it said by other White people) that you "own" x acres of land. But you don't own it; it owns you. Your concept of ownership forces you into thinking like someone who says he "owns" the land: you have to keep official deeds of land in your office safe; you have to fence it off either to keep the bison out or your children in; you have to walk around town all snooty in a cloud of cigar smoke and look down your nose at people who might be worth knowing and talking to; you have to talk like other presumptively entitled people, and even if you're nice or generous, you run the risk of using their words to think and thereby becoming still more and more like them.

In the modern suburbs or exurbs, those x acres of land are represented by your house, the property below it and around it, your automobiles and mortgages on your cottages, all of which demand that you do work for the money to acquire it, maintain it, or "keep" it. Again, it keeps you, and the keeping hides in the words and phrases like "have to."

I remember once meeting a girl named Allegra on the slopes of Squaw Valley (such fitting names). Once we were back in civilization—she in the wealth of San Rafael, me in denim Davis—she extended an invitation to dinner at her father's house, to which I went. It was in the olden times before GPS, but as my Volkswagen Beetle struggled higher and higher into the rarefied air of landed estates on the steep and winding road called Oakdale Drive, I grew nervous. I kept my eyes flicking to my rearview mirror, expecting at any moment to have a police cruiser with flashing lights pull me over. I feared being questioned, hassled perhaps, not shot or cuffed or strangled as he put me in a choke hold and forced me to struggle for breath. That happened to Black people, not Indians disguised by poverty.

Winding upward on that road, the higher I traveled, the more obvious it was that I did not belong there. Wrought-iron gates and fences, high old oaks and rivulets of water that cascaded down and under culverts below the road that might have provided peace if not for my growing apprehension. The broad view of San Pedro and San Francisco Bays from the mountain's top calmed me some by its beauty. When I parked at the end of a circular drive, even my poor Beetle stuttered, creaking with heat and exhaustion so that getting out I felt obliged to stroke its hood and whisper gently to calm it. Why had the girl I'd met not told me she was wealthy beyond necessity or my imagination? Because, to her, in her way of thinking, she wasn't. She would think of herself as well off, not stinking rich, and so well off that she was completely comfortable in her wealth.

A lovely woman who seemed about nine hundred years old, though upright, polite, and with a gracious smile, answered a door the size of the Acropolis.

"Mr. Penn?" she said.

Mister. I'd never been called "mister" before.

"Mrs. Y?"

She smiled and laughed lightly. Silly boy. "No, dear," she said. "I'm Edna. Come in. Here, I'll take your jacket." After hanging it—on a hanger, no less—and hiding it in a hall closet, she led me through the echoes of the entry hall to a paneled room. Opening the door, she said, "The family is in here."

It felt like a boardroom, an inner sanctum. Heavy captain's chairs positioned around a long, polished table, each chair occupied except for the one in which Edna seated me. Silver in abundance, from heavy candlesticks to the three forks, several spoons, and two knives framing delicate bone china plates, with tumblers and crystal wineglasses of varying shapes and sizes—all enough to confuse the savviest of novitiate dinner guests. The family was politely welcoming—a sister and her husband who worked for the head of the table, a son who didn't, two people who seemed unrelated and yet as comfortable as family, Mrs. Y to my right, Allegra across a prairie of polished table. I felt like a boy come to interview for the job of gardener.

Appetizers opened the interview. The family were all nice and polite, very willing to ask me questions about myself and patiently waiting while I made up the answers I thought they might want to hear, answers that would not seem remiss or shiftless. It was not an attempt to lie, to pretend to be other than I was, but a misguided attempt to keep them from feeling uncomfortable. If I took too long replying, Allegra, who was clearly taken with my exotic presence, chimed in with information or qualification that explained my formal jeans and simple no-iron shirt.

"He reads books," she said into the silence that followed my saying I was an English major. "Literature. You know, novels and poems?"

"More fun than mutual fund reports," said her brother-in-law generously.

"Perhaps," I replied. "I don't know. Though there's a lot to be learned from fund reports," I added, wondering why the hell I said that, and in imitation of that bemused tone of mutually assured generosity. For my response I received the tilt of his head and a knowing smile (though what he knew, I didn't). He seemed willing to give to me, and I was willing to give back, but in doing so, I was being disingenuous—lying—in a way that I don't think he was. That is, I felt as though he did enjoy reading mutual fund reports, whereas I never would, believing that literature, storytelling (I remind you these were the olden times), was the be-all and end-all of truth and entertainment.

Slurring her words ever so slightly, Mrs. Allegra said, "Oh, right. What do you think one learns from fund reports other than past performance does not guarantee future results and that you're giving us a shipload of money so we can tell you that?"

"Ma-ma," Allegra said.

Her right hand gripping the stem of her pink gin glass, she laid her left hand on my forearm and said, "Sorry. I just get tired of talking about money."

"I understand," I replied.

She gave me a smile tinged with grimace, willing to believe me yet unwilling to believe that I understood in just that kind of way that she had meant it.

The atmosphere of patient absence of comment was fortunately interrupted by Edna's pushing a serving cart through the doors from the kitchen. On it were small salad plates, each with a quarter head of iceberg lettuce, heavily drizzled over the wedge with a creamy orange dressing. Setting a plate in front of me, she surreptitiously reached down and tapped the handle of my salad fork twice to let me know which fork was the right fork. With five forks, a circus of knives and spoons, and four crystal glasses framing my plate, I was grateful. Picking up my fork, I began to consider how to eat this wedge of lettuce. Mrs. Allegra didn't touch hers, and Allegra sent hers back to the kitchen asking for the Thousand Island dressing to be replaced with oil and balsamic vinegar. I knew lettuce wedges well—friends may well have picked them—and I knew the recalcitrance of iceberg. No sooner would I get my fork irretrievably stuck into the wedge than a chunk of it would split off from the berg like ice falling due to climate change, skip across the slick oil spill of dressing and leap lovingly against my chest or into my lap. The iceberg dexterity of Allegra's sister astounded me and Mr. Allegra seemed hardly to notice that he was eating lettuce at all, as he spoke quietly at the far end of the boardroom with her brother-in-law.

I tried using my steak knife to cut pieces free, jamming the tines of my fork down into the wedge to hold the bugger in place. When I got a large bit free, however, I discovered that the fork had taken root in the wedge, and it took what seemed like minutes to work it free so that I might chase the large bite of lettuce around the plate, hunting it, jabbing at it like a warrior until, finally, I got it.

Then what? Now I had a piece of lettuce stuck on the end of a small-ish fork that was too big to cram into my mouth politely. Worse, I was sweating heavily from the effort of the chase—not perspiring politely like they did. Again, after what seemed like an eternity, I managed to break the chunk down into bites that would just fit into my mouth and, cramming one in, realized that Mr. Allegra had just asked me a question. Did I like D. H. Lawrence?

Shoving the lettuce into my cheek and hoping I did not so much as resemble an overfed chipmunk, I nodded.

Which was my favorite? "If you don't mind my asking," he said, explaining apologetically that he'd taken a literature course at Stanford.

The truth was that I preferred lots of writers to Lawrence. Woolf, perhaps, but especially Bowen. Wanting to please, however, I managed to swallow enough lettuce to allow me to say without spitting Thousand Island dressing across the table, "I suppose *Women in Love*."

"Not *Sons and Lovers*? Funny," he added, "I'd have pegged you for a *Sons and Lovers* kind of man."

Now what did that mean? I wondered, thinking, "Actually, I think I'm more like Mr. Ramsay in *To the Lighthouse* who likes to stand in the front of a rowboat and declaim, 'We perished, each alone.'" Simpering Paul Morel and his hugger-mother had never appealed. "Maybe *Aaron's Rod*," I replied, thinking, "Now I have you." Most readers don't get farther than *The Rainbow*, rarely reading *The Lost Girl* or *Aaron's Rod*.

"That one always seemed a little quickly written to me. If you'll forgive me, sort of tossed off in a way that lets Lawrence make fun of people he doesn't like. What do you think?"

To tell the truth, as nervous as Allegra was about our interaction, I was beginning to think a lot of things. For one, I hadn't expected this. For two, it promised to be interesting. Fun, in a mutual way, but without a fund report to go with it. For three, I was realizing that the rich are not all entitled fools, as a poor boy is apt to imagine, but actually might choose the life they live and that that life is not all emptied out by money and the possession of land. And I was thinking that the part of Allegra I'd been attracted to probably came as much from her father as her mother or sister.

Mr. Allegra ignored the way my salad fork stuck straight up like a semaphore from my lettuce wedge as I began to relax and enjoy myself, surprised that in the middle of their noblesse, a man like him had time to read and think. Finishing my glass of chardonnay as the butler let Mr. Allegra taste the red and then began his round, I began to feel as though I belonged, that these people were not so very different from my people. I smiled at Allegra. Mrs. Allegra placed her outstretched hand over the top of her wineglass and the butler bent to her as she quietly ordered another pink gin.

By the end of the meal, of which I managed to eat enough to fend off half the effects of a red wine that was as full yet smooth as I could ever imagine, when the final glass was filled with a silky cognac whose fire didn't bite but warmed, I thought I understood the rich and why they would not want to give up their riches when a meal with these wines was as usual for them as dropping by Taco Bell or Giant Hamburger was for me. We had talked about literature, touching on Dante's *Inferno* and reaching back to my all-time favorite of *The Odyssey*, agreeing that Milton's Satan was far and away the most interesting character in *Paradise Lost*. I no longer felt like the gardener eating in the big house, and I felt overwhelmingly grateful that they accepted me without comment or criticism, and on my terms of storytelling, and even seemed to appreciate the meaning of my answers to their questions—how did Allegra and I meet? I actually saw myself, a slightly overweight Indian boy, owning a share of this, perhaps even conjoining with Allegra to become as much a part of this family as Mr. Mutual, her brother-in-law.

Dizzy and out of kilter, I'd begun to absorb not only their language but also the attitudes that supported that language. I'd agreed that income taxes were way too high, and I'd betrayed my friends by letting comments about the threat of Mexican immigrants hover freely over the table, barely nodding when Mr. Mutual's wife said that without immigrants the estate's grounds would go untended, and I kept silent when someone advocated the University of California's needing to require students to pay tuition—à la Ronald Reagan—even though tuition was, and ought to remain, free, that the taxes my own parents paid included a forward funding of my tuition, which in turn I would forward-fund by graduating and staying in California, getting a job, and paying taxes of my own. I even accepted an invitation to go shooting with Mr. Allegra, ignoring the trepidation that ran through me knowing that the last time a Nez Perce boy had gone shooting with White folks, he was the target.

All in all, I felt grateful for the apparent acceptance of these people. I was a success. I could tell by Allegra's smiles and the way she tilted her head as though realizing how well a boy could do in her environment if only he tried, and try I had.

But somewhere deep down, my success felt like failure. When I put it truly, I saw how I had failed Grandfather, how I had not resisted speaking like this family of communicants for wealth and favor, and my failure felt bitter. When the butler bent to whisper in Mr. Allegra's ear and he said to me, "I'm sorry, Mr. Penn. I am enjoying our conversation. But I have to take this call," and he slid his captain's chair back and rose, tossing his napkin onto the table, I jolted awake. I don't know if it was the word "have" or the way he said it that woke me. Suddenly I saw how his "land" was his house and the property it was on, demanding the work he had to do to acquire and maintain it, to "keep" it, when in all truth it kept him. If one did not want to "own" all this, then one would not have to work to keep it.

Ashamed of myself, I rose as he rose, and asked to be excused. Gathering up dessert plates and forks despite Mrs. Allegra's protestations and Allegra's shocked expression, I took them into the kitchen to help Edna rinse the dishes and stack them in the dishwasher, store leftovers in containers, and wipe the kitchen counters. Edna was not surprised to see me. Indeed, she seemed rather pleased, and though she did not need my help—I was more of a bother to her, really, as with the energy of a younger woman she moved about quickly but not hurriedly, following an intricate pattern that she must have developed over years—she did not object. When we were finished, she served me an espresso, sat me on a kitchen counter stool, and let me talk, each word and sentence letting off the pressure of shame, she nodding and smiling without judgment or comment or question.

Allegra poked her head in to ask if I wanted to stay the night, and left. I was tempted until Edna laid a wrinkled, bony finger on my forearm and said unwaveringly, "You should go."

"Go?"

"Back to where you belong."

"What about . . . ?" I began, indicating the doors to the dining room, not wanting to be ungrateful or rude to my hosts. Not wanting to be mean to Allegra.

"I'll take care of it. I'll say you felt ill. Suddenly," she added, as if suddenly ill was different from slowly ill, the feeling that had been coming on for the last hour. "Don't worry. They won't care." The way she said the words made me realize that I was far from the first test case dragged home by a slightly rebellious Allegra. She pointed me toward a side door to her kitchen, which let me through and out the front doors without running into anyone, though I could hear the strident undertones of Mr. Allegra taking his call behind his office door.

My poor VW Beetle seemed happy to see me as it waited nervously in the stabled gaze of Cadillacs on the circular drive. Slipping down the long drive, the car began to feel at ease and turning right down Oakdale Drive. I kept it in gear, my foot poised on the brake, trying not to become distracted by the glittering panorama of lights along the bays below while trying to forget the words used to justify lowering taxes while banning immigrants and the covenants that made you accept that language as well as overnight parking on streets, or pickup trucks and travel trailers, or lawns that grew too long or seedy and gardens unpruned and unshaped hedges.

I did not feel good about running out on Allegra. But we not only came from different worlds, we also saw the worlds we came from differently. She imagined that power was wealth and gaining possession, whereas I thought real power lay in not having to, and I believed the power not to "have to" was more substantial than wealth.

It was an idea worth holding.

So when Bean emerged from the scrum of after school into the padded coat and winter hats of the Midwest, arm in arm with Arleigh and DeVon, three musketeers who survived another day's banality, she took one look at the scowl on Mrs. Arleigh's face. Now Bean understands more than one might think, and ever since age two she has said things that astonish. Her parents are very verbal, as is her nana, and last week, when she was limping on her right foot, which was puffy from stitches, and I asked if it hurt her, she sighed and said wearily, "No. It's just that it's so unwieldy." Taking a look at Mrs. Arleigh, watching Mrs. Arleigh's eyes flicker to and from her bumpa as Arleigh said goodbye and DeVon joined the line of after-care kids headed across the street, waiting until we were walking away, once again alone, she asked, "What is wrong with Arleigh's mother?"

"I think she was annoyed by me," I reply. "But I'm not sure." I am, but these qualifiers, these moderators, seem appropriate when talking to the friend of Mrs. Arleigh's daughter.

"Why?"

"I don't know."

Bean gives me that upward glance she gives me when she knows I'm either kidding or not quite telling her the truth. This she understands as well.

I go on. "I'll have to make it up to her, huh?"

"Want to? Or have to?" she asks. "You said that the trick was to know the difference between 'have to' and 'want to.'"

"And all the nuance in between," I say, taking hold of her offered hand.

BALLS AND BUMPAS

"Bumpa?" Bean begins, changing the subject, overwhelmed by the steam of seems. "What was your daddy like?"

"Fuck," I think. "Do I have to?"

And then mentally I change the f-word to "balls," a concession to my father's memory and the manner in which he could make not swearing sound like a threat echoing out of hell itself. "Oh balls!"

Clara's round, open, energetic moon face framed by the wisps of light brown curls pulled loose from the elastic head ties by the jumps and bows and pliés of her dancing to *Swan Lake*—she's Odile, of course—make it impossible not to grin with the breadth of an early dawn before I pushed my lips together and ask again, "Do I have to?"

Do I really have to?

It's all so complicated. "Subtile," the word I've loved for decades because of its "i," giving the modern "subtle" the airy, sticky feel of a spider's web. Follow one strand and you find your thought entangled in another and then another until all you have is a sticky glob of goo and you're left shaking your fingers, trying to get free of them all as you wonder if you loved your father and if he loved you, knowing that somehow you must have thought finding the husk of that love is difficult and requires that you make assumptions that are nothing more than that, assumptions, based on what is now—the love I feel for that upturned face of my always inquisitive granddaughter—and what I know to be true—the love that shows through in her question: she wants only to know her bumpa as well as she can and may; much of what she may love is up to him. Reason enough not to swear, I guess, and definitely reason enough to try to tell the story with love, wherever I draw it from, whatever well I dip the bucket into.

We hardly need yet another disquisition of an unquiet mind on the subject of love, and besides, I am no Cicero. Nonetheless, I lecture my creative writing students on the idea of love, on I. B. Singer's saying that without love there is probably no story worth its effort, that there is little that is without some form of love that matters and manages not to consume your soul like hatred. Only love allows room for human character and justice, and for seventy years—well, for the years since preparing to rear my own family—I've felt nothing in regard to my father beyond fear. Fear of his changeable nature, his being understanding at one moment and then switching to his refined brands of violence. Understanding my knocking over a can of motor oil on his new pebble-dash driveway and yet turning on me when I broke the overhead lightbulb in the garage waving semaphore flags in an assiduous practice aimed to please no one but my father.

I never knew. Existentially, I never could expect a consistent response based on my understanding of the past. So I approached him prepared to duck, to bob and weave or dash into the bathroom where I could lock the door. Or else I waited to tell him about the broken bulb until I was outside in front of the house with the escape of sidewalk nearby. Not wanting to be like him, I've spent a good deal of time teaching myself to keep my face as blank as possible, telling myself that should Clara break something with her awkward pirouettes and pliés, it is an object and it does not matter in comparison to her and to the joy she is so carelessly expressing.

This time and determination has left me certain of one thing: I am not allowed to lie to Bean, though I am allowed the rhetorical interpretation of what might or might not be appropriate. Does a bumpa introduce into the secure foundation of this child's worldview the uncertainty of failure and dissolution? Or meanness or what perhaps was just frustration so pressurized that it exploded at unexpected moments? Does one try to find a way to forgive what he hopes will never have to be forgiven by Clara Bean?

"Bumpa?" she says. She knows. She can hear my thinking. "What's wrong?"

"Nothing. Nothing is ever wrong when you are in the world."

"Then what?"

I think a moment more, then grin. "Help," I say. That's what she says when asked a question she cannot answer. She thinks in a way that shows the grind of gears working and then, giving up, says, "Help." And she is helped.

I've written about him before, elsewhere, but because the writing has lacked love, I feel that it lacks a significant amount of justice as well. I can't say that I feel love for my father, for his memory, for his having been in the world, although I do feel myself continuously afraid of becoming too much like him. I am tempted to dodge the question, except that this is Clara Bean. To know Clara Bean is to know love, just as it was to know her mother and uncle, and that love carries with it responsibilities. So I cop to my default: make it more of a story and try to shape what needs shaping.

"Once there was a young Indian man who decided he loved an English maiden hidden away in the cement and citrus forests of the City of Angels," I begin.

"One night he took her on what back then was called 'a date.' Parking on a gravel turnout above the Hollywood Hills, he refused to take her home until she agreed to marry him, which, tired of being the object of young men's pursuits and without too many other prospects of her own, she did. He was not uninteresting. He was exotic. He held in his wallet prospects for rising employment. Her own father, who was rich, had told her it was getting to be time that she take on responsibilities without his help. She did not stop to think that when her father saw the Indian in this young Indian man—actually saw his broad face and skin toned by sunlight and generations of duskiness—he might be less than pleased.

"In fact, he was so displeased that there was no wedding, only an elopement with almost no contact between her father and his second wife and the now married young couple. Cut off, disapproved of, the bride-to-be and eventual mother began to blame her new husband. After all, people like to blame someone other than themselves. It makes the blame game easier.

"Anyway, they managed to make a home for themselves, moving

into a massive apartment complex intermingled with green space (which back then was called 'lawn'), three patios away from the young man's father and mother and the strange, weird really, persons who seemed to show up unexpected on the grandfather's patio as though it were their destinies. She liked his father who, though he thought much and said little, seemed content to listen to her timid complaints about his son; she did not like his mother much, the way she spent so much time over her slow roaster making enough food to feed them as well as any of the dusky weirdos who might appear. She seemed bossy and unwilling to entertain the idea that her son was less than perfect.

"Of course, he was. Though he had a good job and he was smart, he was not good at getting along with people. He wanted to be included in a hail fellow well met sort of way and yet was neither hail nor well met, and he oftentimes grumbled aloud at the shenanigans of men in white shirts and ties and women in tight knit dresses around the upturned kegs of drinking water near the receptionist's desk. Ere long, his colleagues began to avoid him, walking away from his approach like sneaks before the formless fetid air of a nasty fart, and when the poor man came home and sought his wife's consolation and counsel because he felt hurt and confused by his lack of acceptance, all she could spit out between her tightening teeth was that if he wanted to rise, he should keep his head down and his mouth shut and smile.

"They had kids. Three. Two healthy girls who as babies weighed as much as bowling balls, and a final no-more-sex-after-this son who spent the first months of his life struggling to breathe filtered air in a plastic tent."

Bean's face snaps up at me, a question written all over it. Not who. She knows who. Not even what. What is standing beside her. But where, as in *Where are we going? How are we going to get there?* She's too young for the joke I developed in high school that the mother copulated with the father two and a half times, purposely misquoting Chief Joseph with "I will sex no more forever."

"The father grew frustrated. At work, frustrated because he knew he was equal to or better than his colleagues at doing the work of the workplace. At home, because his wife seemed increasingly angry and distant, and as the children grew, they grew in her direction. She grew more adept at taking out on food what she wanted to take out on her husband for his failures at work as well as the sheer failure of being Indian. They, the pair of them, were different.

"In a last-ditch decade-long attempt by a confused Indian man to be treated like White, the father turned conservative, first deciding small things, such as cursing, were bad. He developed an ability to say 'Oh balls!' with the threatening depth of a natural disaster. Despite all the evidence that people who swear live longer and often happier lives, he made his final journey from defending peoples' rights to be human to defending his privilege to be right. Always.

"Eventually hanging the meat of his message on a Rush Limbaugh skewer of anecdote, the father in his frustrations moved from preachy liberalism to a preachier and angrier conservatism wherein 'things only seem to change but don't, really.' He took up the Bible with a vengeance, imagining himself a St. Paul writing letters to people who either couldn't read or couldn't care, like his children, who kept what distance they could, fearful of being hoisted on another of their father's petards. Even in college, they heard so often the contents of St. Paul's epistles that the words became banal, a thrum against both sound and sense. The eldest daughter turned to marriage, the second to history, and the genetic sort-of son to a love of stories and storytelling that apparently had nothing to do with the Bible.

"All three moved away, as far away as they could, putting the excuses of time and money between them and awful visits with their father.

"'Don't mention x or y,' one child said to another when the discount plane fares of filial duty brought them all annually to town.

"'And definitely, in no way, not if your life depends on it, bring up z,' the other, more in the know, might say.

"'No way I'm having kids,' the elder daughter said, though she was unable or unlikely to succeed biologically.

"'Me neither,' said the second daughter. For whatever reasons, she made her students her kids and, when they were grown and gone, adopted prisoners incarcerated for their convictions.

"What about you, Bumpa?" Clara inquires, and then changes her phrasing with a wink and a nod to "What about the sort-of son?" already recognizing the way "sort-of son" was put, although not quite understanding what its meaning might be. How could she realize that, given that the storyteller had an incomplete idea himself?

"The sort-of son," I reply, not missing a beat, "thought he never wanted to have children. He thought that was the only way to break the cycle that was the father. But one thing led to another and he did. He gave up 'was the only way' and started to think that maybe there was another way, a second, a third way to break that cycle. He, well, not he, exactly, but the woman he wedded, gave birth to a girl, and the sort-of son gave up being sort of and overnight became a grandson of an Indian man, and though he spoke much more than the grandfather—too much more—he began to learn how to listen. Sort of. More, he transformed in the hours of childbirth and first sighting of his firstborn into the worst of massive brown bears who would someday soon knock aside the dead-skin-celled hands of old ladies in grocery stores when they tried to admire the newborn babe in her grocery cart seat, fearing germs and the pollution of talcum.

"It changed him utterly. In addition, it changed the way he dealt with the father, as much as it could change given that such alteration needs to find alteration in the other as well, which failed to happen thanks to the epistolary saints Peter and Paul and the expertise of cheap wines. But he knew, he realized, and he thought and tried to act on the basis of that thinking, that if he was going to break the cycle now, he would have to let his baby daughter love his father in a way no one ever really had and she did because it is normal and usual for a grandchild to love her grandfather if he lets her, and sort of, he did. At least he could lay aside St. Peter with that petard Rush Limbaugh long enough to smile wanly down at the infant when first he visited and it would take him extra minutes to rev his preachy engine up enough to drown out the clarity of feeling in the room that he and the baby occupied."

"Mommy."

"Your mommy. She loved her paternal grandfather. We encouraged that. We gave to him that encouragement, and besides, she saw him only once or twice a year. At best."

"What about Uncle?"

"Ah. Well, perhaps I may summarize your uncle's relation to his grandfather with this."

A story within the story, really, but one that has no beginning and no end, with little in the middle, and yet never ceases to amuse.

"Uncs"—Clara calls her uncle "Uncs" in a deep and compressed affection that they share—"Uncs was pretty young when the father took his collection of epistles and migrated through the door of the afterworld.

"One summer, when your uncs was two and a half, we flew out on the obligatory visit to the father's world, staying fifteen miles north at the elder sister's house where it would be hard for the father to know that we were there for more days than we admitted to him. We wanted to stay and have some fun, at least, while visiting the father on two consecutive days and going silent to disguise our presence if he telephoned on other days. Given the angry, self-righteous way he drove erratically about his own town, it was unlikely that he'd just drop by and surprise us.

"On the first visiting day the father and now the stepmother drove up to sit poolside, ignoring Uncs, who seemed confused by his tone and presence. The stepmother was quiet, content with her own thoughts and imaginings, as the father got his epistolary motor revving and then throwing it into grinding gear brought the message up to speed when suddenly Uncs fell into the pool, causing a disruption and interrupting the sermon, which the father did not appreciate. To tell the truth, it looked to me as though Uncs jumped into the pool on purpose—though I have to admit that the idea of that might be my additive, given how it would make me love him more, if that were possible.

"As the story goes, an acre away a farmer and his combine were harvesting corn in the field overlooked by the yard and preoccupied with the rumble of the tractor, Uncs had misstepped and gone kerplunk into the deep end, bringing me to my feet ready to jump in after him, only to see him dog-paddle to the shallow end, as if he knew what he was doing, where he climbed out of the pool.

"'Oh balls!' the father swore. 'Now look what he's done.'

"'Dad,' the dad said, 'he's not even three.'" I rarely called my father "dad," but in defense of Uncs, I was willing to go to extremes.

"'I don't care how old he is. He needs to pay attention to what he's doing.'

"Maybe he had, huh?" I say to Clara. She seems to know, as I do, that these vague shifts of "dad" and "father," "sister," and "uncs" were getting confusing. I paused for breath and then went on. Once begun, I had to finish, the way I did when my sisters would ask the youthful, eager brother to tell them and their friends a joke, and lacking a punch line, I'd begin the process trying assiduously to find a way to make it funny, suspecting that the way my sisters and their friends were locked in an audiential hilarity was because of my anxious, childish ridiculousness and not because of my joke and yet pleased that they were laughing, not crying or falling asleep.

"'Come here,' the father ordered the boy, as though inviting a dog into his lap.

"Uncs did as ordered, warily, like a boy ready to run for the bathroom and lock himself inside. The father felt the boy's shorts which were still dripping. 'Oh balls!' he exclaimed, 'he's all wet. Now you'll have to change his clothes. You do,' he said, turning on me, 'have spare clothes for him?'

"'We do,' I said, feeling the old fear and subsequent anger well up inside. I didn't challenge the Old Man by reminding him that it was sunny and hot, the central valley of California in summer when the heat had passed 10 on the Head Ache scale an hour earlier. Uncs would dry out quickly, if he didn't scald from the heated water on his clothes. Wasn't like he was going to catch cold. All I'd have to do was strip him, change his diaper, and lay out his clothes to dry.

"The father took hold of the child's skinny arm and shook him. 'You really must learn to behave. If I were your father, I'd—'

"Before he could finish, Uncs took a long look at the father's reddened face and with surprising strength tore his arm free from the father's grip and made a dash for the house, where he jumped through the glass doors, swung one closed on himself, and, in full view of everyone, whipped out his tallywacker and peed on the linoleum floor."

"Uncs did that?"

"He did."

"Peed?"

"On the floor. In full view. The commotion it caused was worth every moment of the Father's apoplectic anger, let me tell you, diverting St. Paul for longer than it took to mop up the puddle of pee."

"That's Uncs," Clara says gleefully, making a little skip and jump and then waiting for me to catch up.

"The real kicker, though, the pièce de résistance, came the next day when we drove down to visit the father in his new house and let him treat us all to an early dinner at Abe's, a diner not only on the other side of the tracks but on the other side of the interstate as well, a cheap diner that splashed up grease fried with breaded chicken and coleslaw made from the culled cabbage from Safeway, and knowing how much he objected to paying restaurant prices over the boxed wine he could have served us at home, we would all order specialty wines or beers. Two, for me, which made me feel all brave and grown up.

"Back at the house afterward, as payment for our dinner, we had to sit about listening to the saints epistle all over the floor as usual, drifting off when we could to the bathrooms or into the passage between the rarely used kitchen and the dining area to inspect the latest curios in our stepmother's curio cabinet. We liked our stepmother, generally, and felt sorry for her having to live with Our Father; before too long, the living room was empty except for me and the father and Uncs who began to handle things. You know, pick up decorative dishes that should have been filled with almonds or cashews, caramels or baby

Almond Joys, and which caused Our Father to shout at Uncs about touching things that were breakable and not his to touch and how valuable that thing was and put that down before you drop it, until I suggested that I help him power up his shiny new walker and we go out back to sit in the arboreal shade of the strip of patio behind this crowd of home. There Uncs could potter about in his diaper pull-ups and Father could stop yelling at him, and if he needed to pee, he could duck behind the peonies.

"Father was proud of his new burp of backyard. Laid out in geometries of rose and rhododendron and narcissus, they all became new causes for him to yell at Uncs who liked the feel of leaves and petals. Father had just had Manuel and Juan of That Juan's Landscaping Services put in a wide bordering frame of redwood mulch to complete the 'easy' of the easy-care yard, and he was proud of having gone to the expense, because pride in expense is what cheap people feel. Uncle tumbled off the low deck and went out to inspect the mulch, tentatively digging his feet into the inches of softness.

"'Oh balls!' the father muttered. 'Those borders cost me a fortune.'

"'It's mulch.'

"'You and that kid of yours. You never will understand, will you? Stop that,' he shouted at Uncs. 'Don't you dare go making a mess of my borders,' he growled in a voice that was all too familiar, low, threatening, on the edge of a smack from the back of his hand could he but reach him. 'Would you stop your damn kid? Look at what he's doing.'

"'He's yours, too,' I thought to say, 'though I hope he'll end up less yours than I fear.'

"'If you don't stop that,' Father shouted, 'I'm going to come over there and make you regret it.'

"Uncs, two and a half, reached a similar end to the end I reached when at seventeen I looked Father in the eye and said coolly that if he hit me, I was going to hit him back. He stepped out into the open, wobbled, then gathered his balance with a sly grin spreading across his cherubic face, dug both feet deep into the mulch and then scooted across the yard on imaginary railroad tracks before levering himself up onto the deck and dashing past us into the house. Father took a swipe at his diaper as he passed but missed.

"'Look at what he's done,' Father said.

"'It's mulch, Dad.'

"'You really must do something about that boy of yours. He's practically . . .'

"'I will, don't worry,' I said, grinning, thinking about telling the story of Uncle and the shreds of mulch.

"And that was my father, your great-grandfather," I say, seeing from her grin that she understands that this story has gone from my father to her uncs, to the utter love I felt and feel for his spirit, for his refusal to take what the father was handing out.

The love I feel for his refusal ever to take anything *his* father might try to hand out as well.

FREE LOVE

Clara Bean wants a puppy. DeVon's female Cairn terrier has littered, and he has offered to give her one of the runts. She is so excited over the prospect that she hardly is able to dance, falling off her tippy-toed pliés to flat-footedness, grounded by her dizzying desire.

Her main argument, indeed her only argument, for getting a puppy is that it would be free, an argument that is difficult to overcome by stealth and manipulation because free is free, as DeVon keeps reminding her. "And it will always love you," he says.

Despite the quibbles I have with the word "always"—there will come a moment where the no-longer puppy but muzzle-graying dog will become so incontinent as to suffer great shame and embarrassment whenever it poops or pees its bed that she and, no doubt, I will feel obliged to drive it down to the vet's and have it euphemistically put to sleep as we hold it and stroke it with comforting farewells as the old dog gives us one long-lasting romanticized look and slips across the "Rainbow Bridge" to a place where, according to the vet's sticker on the plastic urn in which they return scoops of doggie ashes to owners a last time, we will one day meet again. "We," if by then I haven't found my own way into the afterlife, and Bean's "always" being loved by Bumpa will have processed from an always future to an always remembered and yet continuing-to-change past.

The dog pound is run by Christians, I suppose, who believe in things like Rainbow Bridges and not worm-infested mounds of dirt scattered with a packet of ashes that are a hybrid scoop of dust from the pile of dust that comprises all the dogs incinerated during the same eight-hour shift. Not unlike human remains from the incinerators of mortuaries.

"And it's free," Bean reminds me as I wander at her side thinking how to honor her parents' wishes not to have a pet that tracks into their home germs and dirt on a daily basis.

"You'll have to take care of it."

"I know," she says with all the joy and expectation of someone who definitely does not know.

"House-train it. Clean up the mess when it fails to make it outside to go potty. Take it for walks on cold winter days. Teach it not to run out in front of moving cars and trucks in a facsimile of the games of tag that squirrels play with flattening death.

"Sorry," I finish, realizing that Bean has no real truck with death itself. And shouldn't. It's just that the closer one gets to it—the more the evaporation of the self, to the end of the processes that make the self a self, and demand that if one is to have any kind of afterworld or after-life, others who loved the dead self continue to tell stories that remake him in ever more iconized or romanticized, palatable ways—the more one becomes relaxed about talking about the evaporation. And why? Is it just that old people feel required to become deadly dull?

"You'll need to feed it and take it for walks and play with it even when you don't feel like playing."

When, I wonder, has Bean not felt like playing? Play is not only what a child does, but it's also what a child should do, without the sense of going to work at the place called Day Care or Practice or After Care, which latter is a misnomer that seems to embody an ironic sense of what it actually is, and without the rules and regulations that adults seem to think will make not their but other people's children behave like little adults who are as uncivilized as they are when they speed up to prevent someone changing lanes in front of them or curse at students in white Maserati Ghiblis as they drive erratically beyond their lanes.

"I know."

She is confident that she does know. But she doesn't.

But then does any of us ever know?

Seriously. Back in those fabled and over-blamed sixties (which were really just a continuum of the fifties that didn't happen until the early seventies), many of my cohort claimed to believe in free love. They thought that one could have sex with another without consequence or concern or conception and risking only an STD or two. Each of them could part the next morning and go their separate ways, even meeting up at a "happening" without letting on to some bond or historical past existing between them. Remarkably, some of my male cohort seemed to succeed in this and their number of sexual partners would make a Harvey Weinstein envious, as if girls could smell the desire and the freedom that would follow the realization of that desire.

Not so with Bumpa. Even as a young man, he needed to believe that this girl was the One Girl before he shyly accepted her offers of dalliance. He can still remember turning a girl down when she offered to share her sleeping bag with him, partly because it would be too crowded and partly because his inherent shyness did not instruct him on how to proceed with the cool aplomb of his compatriots. He can remember comforting Claudia Colvey without comfort or release because she was a friend who needed holding and she asked him to play that role, sneaking away in the middle night because of his desire to do more than hold, fearful of seeming or being importunate. Claudia might be beautiful, but she was not the one just as he wasn't the one for her either.

Eventually, Bumpa decided that unless he thought that eventually he might marry the girl he dated, he would not and could not pursue her. At first he envied his cohort who could and would. It seemed so easy. But then, as he heard them talk about keeping their options open, he realized that he did not want options. He did not want to be recruited and signed and then later run the risk of being traded away during trading season. Part of this may have derived from the fact that divorce and remarriage seemed a process well ingrained in his immediate family, but most of it was his timidity, his shyness around girls, the fact that as a fat boy in glasses in a time when "fat" meant slightly overweight and not what it means now—as in requiring two seats on a Delta Airlines flight—he would eventually become a person who encouraged female students to "marry the fat boy in glasses."

Why? Not because of himself. Because he realized that as a slightly chubby boy in glasses he'd always tried hard to be funny or intelligent or interesting, not funny ha ha but funny with a positive outlook on the expected future, not intelligent as in pompous or persnickety, not interesting as in knowing which rock singers were au courant but in realizing that Aristotle and Plato had a good deal to say about how to be, and how teaching Bob Dylan as "poetry" was, though Dylan was possibly "poetical," nothing like the real thing of Stevens, or Bogan, or Roethke in which "My Papa's Waltz" was a poem about the love and difficulty between a beloved father and treasured son and not a poem of "abuse," as apoetical students seemed to want to believe, trained as they were to see abuse beneath every cockroach rock or crevice. "Well, he drinks," they'd say, as though that proved abuse, to which I want to reply, "I would, too, if I had you as my dullard child. Lots and lots. Liters."

The fat boy with glasses is painfully aware if he is aware at all of the fact that he is not the ridge-bellied roundhead who attracts the female eye, and thus he has to make himself into being a person nice to know. The fat boy in glasses, in other words, develops not his abs but the muscles of his memory and imagination, revealing his character. And—and—he is dependable and steadfast. He will be glad to be able to give love, and he will feel resolute gratitude at feeling love coming his way (not "returned" like a garment to Macy's but given like a gift, freely and without restriction). Out of the foundation of his character, he will last and not reach toward some absurdity in which he says or thinks, "She just doesn't satisfy me anymore," when satisfaction is not dependent on the other but on the self. Out of the foundation of his resolution, he will look for ways to accommodate—and every pair and couple needs continuous accommodation where there are not mutually satisfying habits. He will at first suspect and then know that the sixties complaint about habit and convention is a false one, that habits are good and conventions are necessary because habits give freedom to act within their continuous framework and conventions give connection and meaning within theirs.

When you marry the fat boy with glasses, be forewarned: you may still be married to him forty years later and maybe even happily, like Babs and Herbert Walker or Michelle and Barack with a mother-in-law who at the farthest lives on or across the street (as mine does) and is, despite that she sometimes drives you bonkers (as mine does), always welcome at your table.

When you marry the ridge-bellied roundhead, be equally fore-warned: his vanity may know no bounds, and you will always have to worry that that woman is interested in him and trying to undercut the habits and conventions that are part and parcel to your marriage. Indeed, he and this other woman, unlike Hamlet, know "seems"—they seem supportive like the cables on a suspension bridge, they seem sym-pathetic where there is complaint to sympathize with, but the only "sym" they feel is with themselves and the rest of the time are essen-tially pathetic. Never leaving the cave, they sit watching the reflection of their own limited selves, unaware of the process of reflection that turns everything not shadowy but fluidly nuanced, depending on what light there is or what light they bring. They do not know the Chi-nese character *cháo qǐ cháo luò* (ebb and flow) or the fact that without ebb you can't ever get flow or that every flow must one day mani-fest ebbing, which is why the moon plays so prominently in romantic fables. Vain people are so vain that they believe that there are such things as entities that are not actually processes, and so they pose, as statues, as cave-bound reflections, not as living beings.

If they overcome their vanity—for whatever cause or reason—they may become frustrated with the superficiality that comes their way: I had one young student who was so handsome as to make other men feel invisible who complained bitterly of the texts and messages he got from female strangers living next door, at parties, or following him down the street to his home. And except for the fact that I felt sorry for this young Adonis and could provide no counsel worth the counselor, I found it ironic that he longed for what I had despite the fact that what I had may seem to be conventional.

Convention as a framework is not unlike the framework of house-training a puppy. You have to work every day to kindly reprimand or correct. Both of you have to work, not one: you may order a puppy, even swat him, but a swatted puppy will eventually give up and simply try to bite the hand that swats him; it's not unlike the abused child who eventually, with uncanny determinism, becomes an abuser. One person may not see him- or herself as "right" and train the other to concede to that rightness—you don't teach a puppy not to poop, you slowly move the newspaper closer to and then out the door so that he accepts the place to go poop. And then you praise him. You don't beat a child into submission, you show him how a person who is nice to know behaves and gradually move the newspaper closer to that kind of behavior, praising when successful, gently guiding when not, as in Clara saying, "I want more oysters," and her mother asking her how she needs to say it, meaning to add a supplicating "may I" tone and perhaps a "please" or two. You don't control the budgets—and often the more successful budgets have one person in essential control, though they may talk about the larger decisions; you realize that everyone likes pin money (if they are lucky enough to have money to be called pin and not food or rent like the mistreated poor in this country) and so you provide equal amounts of funny money for each to spend at will and without consultation within the framework of the necessities of sustenance, shelter, and shoes. Ebb and flow.

And struggle. Sometimes contention.

But consider this puppy thing. What makes a puppy your puppy, what allows you to love this puppy the way Clara would eventually? The continuous effort, the housebreaking, the walking, feeding, caring, petting, and comfort from having it on your lap. The effort—the process of helping your puppy be your puppy as opposed to someone else's—is what creates the loving bond between you and it, just as being fed and cared for, brushed and cleaned and walked, is what makes the puppy instinctively—a puppy lacks language and therefore lacks logic, not unlike unread and ill-instructed human beings, and the ability to analyze and understand that it is the firelight behind them that casts the shadow on the cave wall—recognize the smell and movement that is the you he is overjoyed to see come home because he's lonely / hungry / has to pee or poop.

So effort makes the bond of love. And between humans, love is not shared or reciprocated; it is one directional. He loves a person and he acts lovingly toward him or her. She loves him, in her way, and behaves as though she loves him. But she, nor he, does not "reciprocate." There is no tit for tat, only love in whatever actions either is capable of or desirous of doing. Indeed, reciprocation is one of the conceptual problems that can lead to divorce. When the lover measures what the other shows that she feels, he may find it insufficient and, comparing that with his own head-over-heels love, find it wanting and thereafter begin to introduce concepts like "support" or "completion." Yet love is not a closed circle, a thing. It is a process, a showing, and each of us is helpless before the feeling. Even if we feel the inadequacy of the love coming our way, all we can really feel is resentment combined with a sorrow that begins to poison that which goes from us to her and eventually ends up in two shadows bumping into each other inside the cave until one seeks out a lawyer and initiates separation and divorce (if married) or painful division (if unwed).

Thus, while we may say that there is a "relationship," that relationship is a process, an ebbing and flowing, not an entity in and of itself. I had a student who once blurted out in class that she loved her boyfriend because he loved her, and I instantly felt sorry not just for him but for her as well. But then she was one of those aggressively loud and obnoxious people who saw the world as centered on herself, on what she felt coming her way, and not on what she might or could feel going from her to the world at large.

She was not unlike the graduate student who complains about sexism if a man dates a girl three years his junior, as though three years were twenty and as though the difference in age measured anything more than her sense that she is getting older and her boyfriend might start looking around for others to love because secretly she thinks he is just that shallow and his supposed love for her is just that conditional, on things like appearances, things like the shape of shadows on Plato's cave's wall. Rather than be happy in her love for him, she is happy mainly in his gestures of love for her. While that might be a kind of love (I truly don't know), I would have believed her more if she had said, "I show my boyfriend that I love him as much as possible."

The truth is, then, that love—whether puppy love or love for another human being—is sacrifice, which means to make sacred. It is effort, sometimes painful and sometimes joyous and sometimes matter-of-fact effort. It is a process that must be engaged in continuously without expectation of getting something in return. This process requires self-abnegation, a giving over to loving, not to an imaginary entity of "love," to a gerund, not a noun.

It is for this reason I know that Clara does not "need" a puppy. She is one of the most loving human units I have come across outside of her mother, grandmother, and uncle or father. For Clara loves. Free and freely. She loves DeVon. She loves her better teachers. And, though she asks nothing back for that love, she gets plenty of it herself because she is lovable.

Though she might also get a puppy. And though the puppy would be "free," the effort of raising it to be a puppy worth the having would not be easy but would cost a good deal.

Revelations

B
ean wants a story. I don't have one, but she's insistent, and, well, she's Bean.

"One day," I tell her, beginning, "two anthropologists were out in the Sonoran Desert intervening, because that's what anthros do—they intervene as though poking their noses into places they aren't real welcome will solve problems. They were arguing about whether characters develop or not as they distractedly tapped and poked their hand-carved walking sticks into crevices behind boulders and holes that seemed dug into the dirt thousands of years ago, perhaps by small rodents, the ancestors of the modern Congress.

"'What about edification?' Lycra demanded. She felt stewed by her companion who just could not see the truth behind the things they were saying. It should be noted that Lycra was trained first as an edificationist, the sort of person who goes into children's classrooms and tells them what to think by intervening in their common sense. 'Doesn't a character change with edification?'

"'There's inside character and outside character,' Natty replied. His name was Natty Nostrum, named by his mother's love for Cooper's *Leatherstocking Tales*.

"Nostrum paused, slip-sliding into what you might mistake for thought. Unctuously, as though to insult slightly the way Lycra wanted to stretch her point of view to enclose the whole of the subject, he said, 'Perhaps we ought to think of it as personhood and external reaction to circumstances.'

"He poked his walking stick into the shadows nested behind a boulder, tapping the ground with a dull rhythm, receiving in response a high hissing as though several Rattlesnake babies had been napping in the cool shade offered by the boulder and minded the disturb—, sorry, the intervention into their naptime. Nostrum and Lycra reeled backward from the warning of the hisses. Just last year an anthro known to both of them and liked by one of them had reached a bare hand behind a rock like this only to be bitten thirteen unlucky times by baby Rattlesnakes, which would not have killed him if he had been of taller stature and had not panicked and run to get himself help. As it was, it was only after students mentioned that their professor had not shown up to anthro class on the campus of the college for several weeks that other anthros, always eager to go in search of answers, found his rotting corpse out in the desert, curled around a Saguaro cactus as though in the agony of birth.

"Memorial services were held, after which the dead anthro was all but forgotten except for the department head's lobbying for a replacement hire and except for the fact that an argument arose among certain edificationists about whether the baby Rattlesnakes had bitten him because it was their nature or because they had developed character enough to defend their pencil-thin selves by sinking their tiny fangs into anything soft and warm that moved. Lycra, who believed to the point of knowing that boys were not by nature runners and jumpers, fell on the developing side of the argument, whereas Natty knew that boys were runners by nature and all that would happen as they grew older was that they would run more, both after and away from or, confused by the current correctnesses of their era, in circles as they chased their metaphorical tales (sic).

"Now, out in the hot sun with Natty, hearing the warnings of myriad baby Rattlers, Lycra bent over as if a sprinter in starting blocks, ready to run as Nostrum cast his eyes about in search of an adult Rattler, wary as well despite their nature/nurture arguments about the hissing, looking around to see if Mama Rattler was nearby, perhaps wriggling home loaded with Field Mice and looking a little awkward and almost pregnant for the load. If she coiled and waggled, the dry hissing of her tail sticking up from the coil's center like a bold finger wagging could mean trouble. Both anthros knew, however, that if she coiled too far from them, she might strike but the striking would fall short and all she would sink her fangs into would be at best the thick leather of their knee-high boots.

"All anthros, Bean, wear boots. It keeps them from trouble. Like Wellingtons in James Joyce's *Ulysses*, they're prophylactic, and there was nothing the pair of anthros wanted more than the protection from troubles that would be afforded by rubbers."

"Out of trouble, you mean?"

"No. From trouble. The heavy boots make it hard for them to move too swiftly and so they are forced to intervene less than they might like, and that is good. For you, for the environment, for the general well-being that we like to imagine as Mother Nature.

"A coiled Rattlesnake is able to extend only one and a half times its length when it strikes, and even that requires a snake that has trained up like Fred Alsop or Harry Askew in the Olympics long jump. If a Rattler coils and threatens you, face it and back away slowly. Eventually it will tire of threatening, uncoil, and skulk away like a bureaucrat.

"Good thing, too, given that knee-high boots don't exactly make good on dashing and darting.

"Anyway, silently a four-foot Rattler slithered out from among the rocks and stopped, looking at the two anthros first with one eye and then the other. It lifted its head and took a sniff with the pit in its head provided by Mother Nature for the purpose of smelling.

"'Whew,' the snake said.

"'Wha'd you say?' Lycra asked.

"'What? I didn't say anything,' Nostrum replied.

"'Well, somebody said "whew," and it must have been you as it wasn't me.'

"'That's a stretch,' Nostrum replied.

"'Careful, bud,' Lycra responded, her mouth pulled downward in a tight frown, knowing full well that Nostrum would mention her elastic character for any reason at all.

"Natty laughed. He was happy to have tricked Lycra into expressing both her character and her response to circumstances simultaneously. Not everyone could do that, neither to Lycra nor as Lycra.

"'Whew-wee,' said the snake, lifting its snout to detect what could only be called the sweat of humans out for a hike. 'You two really give off a smell.'

"'Well, you would, too, if you spent all day out in this sun looking for snakes,' Nostrum said.

"'Doubt it,' Rattler replied. 'I'm cold blooded. I like the heat. Fact is, I often take my naps stretched across a rock in the sun. Warms the old skeleton. Not to mention the sole.'

"'See,' Lycra said, poking Natty in the Bumpo with her elbow. 'Response to circumstance. Cold blooded, therefore liking hot sun.'

"'No way, personhood or, rather, snakehood. It's the way she is. She reveals she's cold blooded by sunning herself in the . . . ah . . . sun.' Natty was worried by the circularity of his imaging and wondering if he might not have either shortened his sentence to 'sunning herself,' leaving off 'in the sun,' or, doing what came more naturally to an anthropologist, adding words like coal to a fire until listeners were deafened by a dull roar.

"'What the bloody hiss are the two of you talking about?' the Rattlesnake demanded.

"Nostrum rubbed his eyebrow, realizing what he'd just heard. Being an educationist, too, he was often a sentence or two slow on the uptake, like hearing a student say something almost intelligent but not becoming aware of the nigh-on intelligence until one had moved on to the next bullet point on the sheet of lecture agendas. 'What's all this about "soul"?' he asked.

"'Just because you wear 'em doesn't mean we don't have them. See?' Rattler asked, rolling slightly toward her side to show off the diamonds on her underbelly, where the skin was toughened by constant contact with the desert dirt and rock. Nostrum and Lycra both jumped back as though threatened. Rattler laughed. 'Not to worry,' she said. 'Just showing you my sole.'

"'A soul isn't actual,' Lycra said. 'Your soul is something you have and don't have. Or have and can't prove that you have.'

"'At least until you go to meet your Maker when you die,' Nostrum added.

"'Not that kind of soul. You're spelling it wrong. I said "sole," as in "s-o-l-e," not "soul" as in "u." Like the sole of your boots. You walk on it. I crawl on mine. As for soul with a "u," who knows until it's way too late to worry about.'

"Lycra, typically, had stopped listening, thinking expansively as she'd been trained to do in graduate school. 'I've got an idea,' she said.

"'Uh-oh,' Nostrum said.

"'Double uh-oh,' Rattler hissed.

"With a restrained annoyed gesture, one a student would not have been sure indicated annoyance had that student been paying any attention to the lecturer not paying any attention to him, focused as she was on edifying him and not encouraging him to surf his data, Lycra ignored Rattler. 'How'd you like to take part in a little experiment?' Lycra asked the Rattlesnake.

"'Speriment about what?' Rattler asked, with a suspicious shake of her hissing tail. It was thinking of coiling and maybe striking one of these two fools just to get a taste of what moved them.

"'About character,' Nostrum said. 'My friend Lycra here thinks that characters evolve and develop. That they don't just respond to altering circumstances but that they learn from the alteration and that changes the way they react and respond because their character has changed essentially.'

"'Snake is not snake when it alteration finds?' the snake said, its tongue flicking at the pair in laughter.

"'That sounds familiar,' Lycra said.

"'It's Shakespeare,' Nostrum said. 'Love is not love . . .'

"'So Shakespeare agrees with me, then?'

"'Come on. You've never read Shakespeare.'

"'Not read per se. But my cousins the Adderlies played tragical roles in *Antony and Cleopatra*, if you read that one.'

"Nostrum, who'd read Cliff Notes on Shakespeare's tragedies and was familiar with the evolution of Cliff's Notes to Cliffs Notes to CliffsNotes, couldn't recall any Adderlies in *Antony and Cleopatra*. But a clever edificationist, he did what he did in front of a classroom when asked about something he didn't know: he changed the subject. 'Love is not character. Love is a process, a feeling that one hardly can help when he feels it.'

"'But the lover loves, and that becomes a part of his character,' said Lycra.

"'Not when he finds alteration. Despite what Bill Shakespeare says, if the lover finds that the loved one despises him, then eventually he will cease to love her if he's smart or beat his head against a border wall if he isn't. Either way, his character only reveals itself. That is, he is either capable of admitting defeat and moving on, or he is stolidly incapable of it and he has to bang it out of his head.'

"'Care to put it to the test?' Lycra asked.

"'How?'

"'So you, Ms. Rattlesnake, do you like to eat Field Mice?'

"'Ye-ess,' Rattler said. 'Even if they are gluten-free.'

"Lycra ignored this obvious attempt to derail her argument. 'Do you think that if we promised to pay you a certain sum you could live in a large area with a family of Field Mice and not eat them?'

"'How much is this certain sum?' To Nostrum, who was tapping his walking stick on a chunk of sandstone, she said, 'Would you stop that? You're making my tongue flicker.'

"'How 'bout a dozen Robin's eggs?' Lycra asked.

"'Two. I've got mouths to feed.'"

"'Two, then,' Lycra replied, sure that she could get a grant from her college to pay for such important research on character and its development. She'd be proven right, and more important, Nostrum would be proven so very wrong, and everyone knows in the world of right and wrong that while being proven right was great for merit and promotion, having your friendly opponents proven wrong was good for the sole as well as the soul.

"Agreement was reached that in four weeks the two anthros would return to this very spot and take up Rattler for her stay in a laboratory that they would bring and set up in this secluded part of the desert.

"Why four weeks? Rattler wanted to know, and Lycra began delineating the various committees and administrators who would have to sign off on such a live-animal experiment, assuring the naturopathologists that no harm would come to a wild animal while biodiversity would be maintained and that after the experiment was finished and conclusions drawn, or at least sketched out in impenetrable language with long, awkward sentences for anyone who cared to investigate them, which, once the annual cycle of merit and promotion was finished, probably no one would do, the college would be able to use those conclusions for fundraising and would own the results (unlike the productions of the creative writing program where the things that were published but no one actually read would remain the property of the failing writers), though most likely it would just ignore all but the line entry on the annual budget that summarized 'research expenditures,' into which the piddling amount for herpetological nature/nurture studies would be folded so easily as to make it transparently invisible.

"The day Natty Nostrum and Lycra returned to make the retaining deposit of six organic, free-range Robin's eggs to Rattler, Natty noticed that the Rattlesnake was distended slightly about the midsection. He simply smiled, held his peace, and said nothing. And once the habitat was set up and the snake family installed, the babies having grown substantially after the intervening four weeks, Lycra and Natty set about convincing a family of Field Mice, six in all, to take up residence in the holes provided by sinking corrugated tubing into the ground in configurations that would make a colony of ants of color seem a simple high-rise apartment complex. After nineteen days, the number of Field Mice darting hither and thither were impossible to count, the boy mice having impregnated the girl mice and the offspring numbering in the tens for each and, being mice with few scruples and fewer morals, immediately copulating with any member of the opposite gender regardless of family or parentage, produced tens of more mice within twenty-one more days until Natty made a mental note to write a brief paper for

National Geographic about the revealed morality of certain species and how Field Mice seemed not unlike Catholic priests in their willingness to entertain the 'other' regardless of age or background or gender.

"Meanwhile, the baby Rattlesnakes grew more quickly after Rattler renegotiated the contract of abstinence and developmental learning curves so that Natty and his pal Lycra were no longer allowed visitations at any hour or on any day but were limited to the sabbatical days of Sunday, Saturday (out of sensitivity to Jews), and Thursday, which is the holy day of L. Ron Hubbard's Scientology wing of modern religious bearing and thought. Very soon, even Lycra began to regret the experiment as Field Mice began to seem everywhere, impossible to count and more impossible to keep track of as the teenage Rattlesnakes, not having been signatories to their mother Rattler's contract with the college researchers, felt no compunctions about grabbing a quick snack on the fly, so to speak, on the dart and dash, doing their level best to digest their snacks before the researchers drove up in their new Land Rover and parked at the edge of the snake-mouse reserve, with Lycra already lamenting how the entire project was being overrun with the squeak and squick of multicolored Field Mice.

"Through all of it, through field research and data gathering where Lycra would stand with a tablet computer in her hands tabulating while Natty tried to estimate the numbers of mice jamming the tubes and tunnels provided by the government for the mice, using his cellular phone to snap photos of bewhiskered noses poking out of and from behind and out in the open as snakes flickered nearby evidently indifferent but actually sated and uninterested (which is very different from disinterested, the way Mama Rattler was supposed to behave, given her two dozen Robin's eggs), virtually nothing was proven.

"By the end of six months, the Federal Department of Mice and Rodentates had begun to grow curious about the satellite images of this small section of desert just outside the Navaho Reservation, which looked like a small swirl of dust storm from the NASA Space Station, and a senior administrator for NASA met (for that's what administrators do best, meet) with the Head of All Research at the college and expressed his dismay about Natty Nostrum's and Lycra Spandex's 'Revelation and Development Project,' which by then included the two senior researchers and fifteen hungry graduate students needing employment and needing more funding for food and shelter, who were willing to catch, fillet, and fry Rattlesnake meat as desert kebabs, even though the skeletal bones of these fry-ups left them picking their teeth for hours.

"By the end of the year—the academic year, which ended on June 1 and didn't restart until the end of August—there were so many Field Mice that the grad students had given up trying to count them or even estimate their numbers and had taken to drinking and smoking illegal but socially acceptable drugs and hanging out around campfires together, behaving much like Field Mice with their couplings until by late September it was learned that several of the graduate students of gender were pregnant and would produce future students of gender who would grow up (more slowly than snakes or mice) to be able to hold tablet computers and record if not numbers of mice then, well, things of import and as it turned out things of import were all that mattered to the administrators who continued to meet because meetings seemed one of those important things.

"And thereafter, both Natty Nostrum and Lycra Spandex rose in the ranks to become administrators themselves, marking new research projects as 'fundable' as long as the research they did was couched in new-and-improved language with frameworks and rubrics and the whole schmegeggy of three-syllable words that could be framed in the works and make little or no sense to anyone but the researcher and a ten-year-old granddaughter who by now is practicing her stage entrances and exits and pliés for her imagined ballet while every now and then stopping to frown at Bumpa not with annoyance but with a grin of real interest in making sense of whatever the hell he's telling her. She stops, Clara Bean does, and her eyes wide on her round face, asks, 'So?'"

Bumpa, who has been adding and embellishing the way most storytellers do, searching for meaning but, more important, an end that is at least as significant as "And that's how it was"—the Nez Perce way of ending, which recognizes that the end is a lot less important than the process, especially given that all stories essentially could be told "He was born, drank coffee, and died," throwing the emphasis on the part where he drank coffee (or other things) except for the possible, probable, and believable tales of the tripartite Bumpa told after he has finished the third partite and died by a then older-than-ten granddaughter, which gives him the only immortality he can, will, or wants to have when she will conclude not "that was what he was" but "that was how he was" and that "was" was "silly," and Bumpa is nothing to Clara Bean if not silly and silly is good because in silly we learn a lot about how to be and not be too self-interested and serious about it.

"So, what?" he asks.

"What happened to Natty and Lycra? To Rattler and the Field Mice?"

"They revealed their characters. Rattlesnake never really developed but only revealed that her character was to hunt and eat, striking out in the dark at heat and motion, or able to see because of her cat's-eye vertical pupils in low light, never truly abiding by the abstinence contract and able to fool the researchers because of the sheer numbers of Field Mice whose character was, in the case, to propagate and be consumed and digested, not unlike the way rich people think about the poor.

"But more so—and this is the conclusion that neither Natty nor Lycra nor NASA and the college administrators ever came to realize— Natty and Lycra proved that people do not develop. After all, what right-minded thinker would conclude that going from teacher to researcher to administrator who meets is in any way a 'development' or increase. They reveal: for you can only become a college administrator if you have the sole of an administrator from birth and step-by-step you walk on that sole to climb down the path from fertile mountain to equally fertile but difficult-to-discern desert to eat or be eaten or at least bitten, where every meeting, every resolution, every rubric is like attaching another of the Adderlies to your chest until you are bit-ten so much and so often that students of common sense will need CliffsNotes to count the footnotes of revelation."

"You're silly, Bumpa," Bean says, giving my arm a hug.

"That's true. I am."

3

Schooling

A HARVEST MOON

Clara calls me "Bumpa."

"Bumpa," she says, "when I told Ms. Hanson you were Indian, she said you weren't. She said Indian was insulting. You were Native American."

"Fine," I say. "Except that there is no 'American' about it."

"What do you mean?"

"I mean that when Amerigo Vespucci fetched up on the shores of what is now our country, there were only Natives, Indigenous people who had not yet learned the graft and glory of being Americans. True, there are theories that said Indigenous people crossed a land bridge from Asia, a bridge that either never existed or exists no longer, kind of like Sarah Palin's Bridge to Nowhere. But then there are also theories by people without an understanding of metaphor that all of us came from a man called Adam and a woman called Eve, and had the good luck to be evicted from Paradise, which I've always imagined would be like living in Michigan, at two p.m. on a mild fall day."

"Yecch," Clara says. "That'd be boring."

"Not to mention having always to rake up fallen leaves."

"Which is why it's called fall, right?"

"That or it refers to 'fall back' as we Indigenous people turn our clocks back so we're on the same page with Geats and Celts."

Clara Bean frowns. "Bumpa!"

Got her. For the whiffiest of instants she considered the "fall back" business before she recognized that I was kidding.

Clara and I walk to the park, much as I did nightly with her mommy, telling stories of Stuart and Frankie. Stuart is a brown squirrel, Frankie black, and the first time I pointed again at a black squirrel and said, "Look, there's Frankie," she demanded to know how I knew that was

Frankie and I replied with authoritative calm, "He's black, isn't he?" and the logic of it convinced her. Just like her mother.

When she finally figured out that I might be not quite accurate—that brown and black were just squirrelly metaphors—she had stopped caring, too involved with our stories of hunting and storing acorns, or dashing up and around trees like the red on a barber's pole.

Now I have to say, digressively, for those of you whose eyes are riveted to mobile devices and whose attentions don't exist outside of a squirrelly twittering without the recognition of danger, there is no greater pleasure for a bumpa (and by extension a nana, mommy, daddy, uncle, or aunt) than to hold the perfectly formed tiny hand of his granddaughter and walk. Anywhere. To the park or Clara's favorite, the bookstore, is just an increase, though not of name but of being. Oh, and since eighteen months, she has loved Whole Foods because it gives out cheese and bread in small domes of sample tasting. She loves cheese.

"As for Ms. Hanson, 'Native American' is equally as wrong as 'Indian.'

"So she's wrong?"

"Not exactly," I say in the musing, here-comes-a-story voice. I do not want to undercut Ms. Hanson's authority. She is a wonderful elementary-school teacher, underpaid, overworked, hardworking, and serious but cheerful. I couldn't do what she does, and her intentions are as good as any of the well-meaning people who believe that changing the words will change the experience, much of which is historical, already in the record books, so to speak. This old-age thing seems to cramp you all up and constipate you.

Lighten up, Bumpa.

"So you'll come in and tell the class about being Native American?"

Aha. I'm a resource. Not unlike someone who plays the mandolin professionally. Except I am not a professional Indian. I know professional Indians and I don't much enjoy them. Their day books are filled with snubs and verbal injuries that seem to injure the slight. I am as stuck with them as they are with me. I can't put it down and take up another set of attitudes or beliefs. But a resource, that's interesting.

"Sure," I say to Beaner, who snuggles up as we walk and gives me a sideways hug.

"Really?"

"For you, anything." And for the disbelieving, for Bean or for her mother or uncle, I'd do anything legal, up to and including death, with which I have had more than my fair share of experience.

"What do you think I should talk about?" I ask her, expecting her to suggest, in her desire to have everyone enjoy my visit, "feathers and fandango."

But she doesn't. Instead, with all the seriousness only a seven-year-old can muster, she replies, "What you always talk about."

"Which is?" I say, thinking, "Always? Do I always talk about one thing?" You may imagine the anxiety with which I await Beaner's definition of "always."

"Process," she said.

Whew. She's right. I do always preach process. There is no good story, but that it is well told, no good song that is not well sung, no human meaning without love. No joy without contentment, even momentary. No having experience, just experiencing and then remembering the experience in myriad ways as you tell and retell it to others or yourself, and if you don't want your fraternity brothers to pack up their Mickey's Big Mouth beer and leave you high and dry, then you'd better tell your travel experiences well.

Indeed, you may want to add some spice, at least some pepper and salt the way a good cook balances sweet with sour. Even if the spice you add is, well, not quite true. (Here you must pay attention to definitions of realism, as in believable, probable, possible: you may not sleep with a spacecraft alien on the poorer streets of Barcelona, but you may sleep on the sidewalk bunched together with traveling companions for warmth and protection, sleeping in poorer neighborhoods the police, wearing their teeny patent-leather hats, avoid.) If it keeps your reader/auditor engaged, it's worth the cost to fact.

Keep the details consistent, and worry less about "facts" and more about the truth of what the story says and about whom or what. If it is meant to aggrandize yourself in order to pick up girls (or boys), then it is by definition not a story, and you are engaged not with the process of telling a good story but with impressing others with a weak story, often involving money, drugs, or sex. Remember, too, that camera snapshots are, in fact, not factual because the human context of speech, movement, ambient noise, and call and response is not present in that digitized fixity. Snapshots are boring, and no imaginative person wants to look at yours.

There are historical facts: blankets infested with smallpox were distributed to starving, freezing Indians; an estimated sixty million Africans perished in the triangular trade of slave ships; six million or seven million Jews, Gypsies, and other people Ayn Rand would discard in dustbins died in German and Polish extermination camps, but these facts are not stories. You cannot even get at the story. You cannot tell it well, because if you are a human being, your mind is incapable of imagining the actualities. Truths and historical facts are umbrellas for stories, large contexts for the stories that might be made out of the experiences, umbrellas under which teller and listener may temporarily keep dry.

The odd thing—at least odd when I think about it—is that you cannot tell a good story about any of those "truths" unless—*unless*—the story is about survival, not death; love, not hate; and, damn it all, forgiveness. A well-told story even about bad things—and come on, those are pretty bad things mentioned above—must have or offer in whatever complicated understanding and alteration, hope. It must offer . . .

"Bumpa?" Her hand gives mine a squeeze as her engines begin to rev at the gates to the park and playground.

"Process from an Indian perspective, is that it?"

"Yup."

"How?"

Clara darts over to a fallen branch of maple leaves, all reds and golds, and hands it to me like an olive branch.

"Just talk to them like you talk to me."

"I can't."

"Why not?"

"Because they are not you." Beaner slips my hand and runs for the playground where she will spend the next hour meeting, greeting, climbing, joining and unjoining, sliding, and jumping from heights no Bumpa should allow.

Kids are already there with their parents; others will inevitably show up. Though I greet the other parents, I take myself off to a triangular seat corner of the large sandbox to think about playing Indian for Clara Bean's class.

Hanging from a high branch of a tree and swinging a worrisome height off the ground, Clara calls out, "Look, Bumpa!"

A mother named Mary comes over to bend with her scooped-neck sweatshirt, playing Tonka trucks and graders with her youngest. Fortunately, another father with whom she is having an affair shows up with his boy. She unbends and leaves me watching her youngest, who seems unhappy and silently uses an old Barbie doll to beat a Tonka dump truck into submission.

I imagine myself in front of an overload of faces upturned like teacups for the fluid telling of what it means to be Native American. I'm nervous. After all, a few of these teacups are Clara's friends; others are the offspring of helicopters that hover protectively over them; and some—the digitized ones I want to recycle—will be rudely uninterested in anything I might say.

To be introduced—me without feathers or dark aviator glasses or hair grown long and tied with a turquoise studded band into the hair of a horse's ass—as Native American, when really all they wanted to see was some wrinkled old fart in beady leather, and then to launch into a lecture on process will cause even Beaner's best of friends to turn and look at her as if to ask, "What have you done to us?" the answer to which is "Don't blame me, blame Ms. Hanson." Not "Hanson," but "Ms. Hanson."

With that, I have it. Even Mary Bender of the Loud Affair worries at my excitement, as I gently pump my fist, once, like a restrained golfer sinking a twenty-foot putt.

The day arrives. A room mother—a person of no color who feeds on interest in things like Native Americans—asks me what I think of Michigan Indians getting a monopoly on wild rice. When I try to explain that my people don't do rice but pine nuts, she says, "Oh, so just what kind of people are you from?"

"Nu-mi-pu," I say. "The Wallowa Valley."

"Oh. You mean the Nez Perces."

"I guess."

Without effort on my part, I quickly get to know this person. She's a "room parent," a decent, generous, bombastic, pushy, know-it-all kind of loud mother who does good work by helping out Ms. Hanson. The last thing I want to do is enter battle with her or in any way deflate her authority with the kids, who are beginning to mill and grin, fluff balls floating in the winds of our confusing blowhard contention.

"Explorers called them that. Francophone explorers ran across some who decorated their nostrils with bits of blue shell, Gothy piercings that got them thereafter called 'Pierced Noses.' The explorers even wrote it down, so it had to be true."

I could not help but add—I am a lot less than perfect—"Sort of like Nu-mi-pu meeting Catholics and calling them 'Bent Knees.' Or 'Wafer Wolfers.'"

The woman knits her brow, trying to decide if I'm joking or if I've just told her something important about Native Americans.

Ms. Hanson claps her hands twice, and the kids go quiet, turning their attention to her. The room mother melts into the back beside two boys playing video games on handheld screens hidden below their desk. Beaner sits proud and upright, an epicenter of her friends who all sit straight up with their hands clasped on the desk before them, expectant, looking from Bean to Ms. Hanson to me as the introduction promises them all more than I can deliver.

In the interests of diversity or the interest of getting them to start thinking about the fact that Indian people differ in custom and craft,

I've brought a beaded headband, a Hopi pot, a kachina, a Navajo marriage pot. What looks like a tree trunk with a face has the head of
Coyote sticking out from the stomach: Bean's mother's hand-molded
clay sculpture of Ilpswetsich, "Swallowing Monster," from whom Coyote created the Western Peoples—the Big Bellies, the Flatheads, Uma-
tilla, Cayuse, Blackfoot, and others. From the blood of the monster's
heart came the "Pierced Noses," a people of courage and heart, the
Nu-mi-pu, or Human Beings.

"Well, class?" Ms. Hanson asks when I've finished, a moment that
is easily identified because our stories end "And that's the way it happened" or "That's how the Nu-mi-pu came to be."

"That's a stupid story," says Ralph, whose name actually is Tri-Ing
or Vapide. "It's not even true."

How would he know? Even during my telling, he lifted his head only
at Coyote's flint knife, his cutting holes in the stomach wall, the blood
from the monster's heart.

Bean flinches. She's ready to defend Bumpa against anyone. I lift
my hand at my side, a subtle stop signal, give her a quarter frown and
a barely visible shake of my head. *Wait*, it says. *I can deal with this.*

"Well, Vapide, last night Bean, I mean Clara, asked me why the
moon hung so low and loud overhead and had turned so yellow-
orange. You know what I said?"

Vapide is doing his best to look all vapid, but in truth he's a touch
curious. "Dunno."

Bean can't resist. She knows. Her parents have kept her from screens
like congressmen keep away from the Zika virus. She gets the relationship between imagination and the relationships of respect. She raises
her hand.

"Clara?"

"Because the cheese is aging," she says happily.

"That's not true," Vapide says. "That can't be true."

"More like 'won't be.' You're right. It won't ever be for you."

TEACHING SCHOOL

When Clara Bean heard she was starting school in the fall, she spent the summer worrying about her lesson plans. What was she going to teach her students?

Her daddy is a teacher. Her bumpa was a college teacher for forty years. Her paternal grandparents were both teachers. Her aunt teaches, not to mention two great-aunts. Teachers, teachers everywhere and not a lot to think. So it's only normal for Bean to imagine that going to school means going to teach, that the teaching mantle has fallen around her shoulders. It never dawned on her that she would not be the one teaching but the one being taught until with a worried look over a lunch of oy-oys—tinned oysters, which she loves—she told me how she couldn't be sure how to go about teaching at school.

"How should I do it, Bumpa?"

I'm never sure about irony anymore. We live in such an ironical and impossible-to-believe world that it seems as though irony has doubled back on itself to form a Möbius strip where you can follow the surface of irony around as it twists and then twists back again only to end up in the original moment of disbelief. The confusion of politics could make a book on irony. An ironical book.

Yet, casting aside doubt and confusion, there also seems to be a truth somewhere in there. Bean enrolls in school, Bean goes to school, and Bean's teachers, no doubt well-meaning and kind, learn things they didn't know they knew. Such as how a four-year-old girl knows that licorice pronounced incorrectly as "likerish" may also have once meant "lascivious," though that very four-year-old has no idea—nor should she—of what "lascivious" means or might mean to the future of her hashtag.

Given my personal history with teaching—my mother taught, my father dabbled in it after retirement, one sister taught Chicano kids and wrote an early book on the then new Montessori methods, my other sister has taught and gone on teaching even in quasi-retirement—Natives and minorities, especially incarcerated ones, and graduate students who need her help on their committees. My son-in-law, the child of two teachers, is an excellent third-grade teacher and even though Phil McGuire, a long-ago acting interim chair of my university department who got overtaken by his sense of power and purpose, once asked me how I knew someone was a good teacher if I'd never seen him teach, I do know a good teacher from his attitude and energy. From what he says about teaching and how he says it. Philip's stupid question, though he was a very good teacher himself with a strong reputation among the better students, is not unlike asking, "How do you know, having never touched it, that the moon is cold?" or "How do you know that the professor who insists on discussing the importance of *Fifty Shades of Grey* and its meaning in the modern world is probably not a very perceptive teacher?"

You think I'm going to say, "Because it's *Fifty Shades of Grey*." But you're wrong. It's the use of "modern" world as though there is such a thing in philosophical meaning and process as "modern" that is different in its broad strokes from "ancient" or "old" or "former." Like the student who depends on the coat hook of "in the world today," the professor is (1) detached from contextualized ongoing process and (2) shallow and unthinking of the fact that people are not and have not been very different from one another, whether painting on the dim walls of Lascaux or in the sunlit studios of Giverny.

We needed the steel strikes of the 1920s as now we need the teacher strikes of the 2018s and 2020s. Fools continue to confuse their antipatriotic "Love it or leave it" attacks on the dissent and peaceful protest that is at the heart and soul of American improvement and advancement with the idea that NFL players who kneel during the national anthem are not lovers of a better vision of America where Black children are not shot down like carnival ducks by people hired to protect them and us, to uphold the rule of law, but people who do not value the tremendous contribution to our safety by members of the armed services and thus ought to ("love it or") leave it. Who, in this cycle of stupidity, is the patriot of a nation born in revolution and protest against autocratic imposition of rules and taxes and laws that apply only to colonials and not to the privileged in the House of Lords? Who, besides a professor bent on the autocratic illogic of agendas, is more anti-American: the person who wants his rights at the expense of yours or the person who admits to mutual and sometimes variant rights under the law?

Does a professor who cops to "modernity," like the forgivably mindless student in his very distracted "world of today," actually think that people no longer fall in and out of love, fight and make up, that the history of human beings has not cycled through and through and over and over and that while the technologies have changed, little else has, though now it does seem as though some of the technologies are causing the biology of human beings to modify and evolve?

That professor of English, who ought to have read T. S. Eliot's "Tradition and the Individual Talent" even in the excuse of her modernity, should remember that it is Eliot who wrote, "Some one said, 'The dead writers are remote from us because we *know* so much more than they did.' Precisely, and they are that which we know."

If investing (for her retirement, which cannot come soon enough), that professor would be indulging in recency bias, that what has gone up in the past will continue to go up in the future. The bias is equally as dangerous culturally or educationally as it is with stocks. But like their professors, students have been brainwashed to believe in recency bias, that "things have changed," that they are different now from how students have always been. That their stock has been going up and up and up along with their inflated grades and yet there is no bubble and no crash or "correction" that must come after graduation when by entering the world they begin to learn how much they haven't—learned, that is.

There are differences in the euphoria of being youthful: the classroom across from mine seats one hundred students in rows and columns and, when I look in, contains little else but dopamine as students arrive, cell phones in hand, to sit uncomplaining of the cinder-block walls and the regimentation of rows, shielding themselves from thought or meditation with screens. In their convenient absence of complaint or friction against their not always mindful world, you could insist that they are avoiding the trouble of human contact, not unlike women on the NYC subway who bring along thick books with raised foil covers as an excuse to keep their eyes down and avoid the random rapist or crazy conspiracy theorist, but the danger the students avoid comes not from outside but inside. Harm exists out there; aren't we all survivors until we're not? But here in this protected college environment the real harm comes not from the presence outside the self but from the absence inside the self, a hardened shell of agendas filled with a buttery substance that would kill a field mouse.

It reminds me of the birthday "cake" I bought myself the first year I lived in England, which, when I cut into it at home, cracked into pieces to reveal a hardened chocolate shell filled with cocoa-flavored sugar cream; turned over, the "cake" was a hard chocolate bowl of icing without a lick of floury cake inside. As I tossed it into the trash, I wondered why the bakery clerk had not warned me.

At first, I fantasized that it was because England is nothing if not rules of behavior and work, a place where "work to rule" was invented and is pursued with a determination that would win a war. A common laborer can be lifting a shovelful of gravel when the clock's face calls out "time for tea" and he will drop the shovelful and measure his unionized steps to a thermos of Whittard's English Afternoon, pouring out a cuppa before lifting out a small thermos of warmed milk and adding one or two cubes of sugar to taste, stirring with a twizzle stick, and then leaning back against a pallet of cinder blocks to joke and jaw with his pals who have dropped their own shovels or hoses or hods of cement, gabbing about inconvenient road works, warning one another where the A38 hits a construction tailback that would impede their journeys home if any of them were headed to Birmingham.

Lists of road works complete the air like the sunshiny mist that lifts from their shoulders as they wrap up morning tea, and if you know road works in Britain, you know that the worker running the STOP and SLOW octagon, now that tea is over, is about to return to work to help the lines of cars negotiate past one another in bunches. While he was at tea, cars and their drivers have been forced to negotiate for themselves—and only in a nation as civilized as Britain may this negotiating take place in an orderly way, southbound alternating with northbound, one by one, sans honking or intentional cheating. Indeed, in the very center of London, my cabbie has pulled aside to let a car travel a full two blocks down to and past us while the car behind that one has stopped and waited his turn for my cabbie to pull back out and travel through in the opposite direction. In America it would take ten seconds before the entire section of road resembled a used-car lot or a strange twist of accident where some NRA acolyte was shooting up the line with an AR-15.

The rule of civility and politeness, the embedded sense of fair play and generosity is what makes Britain's rulishness not so rulish. Unlike the girl in the Saturday market who did not "do" Gouda when I reached the head of the cheese line, the bakery girl who sold me the cake *had* tried to warn me. Gently, recognizing my American accent and therefore my propensity for violence, she asked if I knew what I was pointing to on the bakery shelf.

"Of course," I said, thinking the picture-perfect round of chocolate icing would contain moist and wonderful cake, probably layered once or twice with additional frosting.

"People do find these a little sweet," she said, assembling a folds-all cake box and sliding the cake inside. "But," she added, smiling a wan, thin smile as moist as the springtime air outside, "it may be just the thing."

"I'm sure it will."

I, in my determination, ignored the voice inside my head asking, "British people find something too sweet?" These were a people whose idea of cinema popcorn was a bagful of popped corn with sugar freely laced over it. Unfamiliar with hard cake-size shells of chocolate filled with ganache, unaware that they existed in the world, I ignored her smiling resignation and gentle hinting with the same certainty with which my students ignore my warnings about addictions to cellular phones and the vagaries of the bot-infested internets. I did not listen to her, the same way that a good half of my students say their professors don't listen to them.

After all, their professors profess only to care about education. Willing to submit to lesson plans, rubrics, and outlines, statements of "outcomes" and "skills" that strangle out the life and actually reverse the processes of education, the professors have already accepted that what they do in their classrooms has nothing—nothing—at all to do with education, only with agenda and edification, right thinking (as defined by each of them), and the possibility of guessing right to get a job in a rapidly changing economy. Their agendas are propositions, proscriptions that they deem worthwhile or moral or beneficial. They are not processional. They do not ask students to think about an idea or subject, possibly even to argue with them, but only to agree and regurgitate.

And therein lies the problem, Clara's and mine. We worry over lesson plans. She, because she imagines the plans will let her guide her teachers and friends; me, because I worry over guiding anyone anywhere, worry over doing more than derailing the parallel tracks of assumptions the students have acquired from teachers of certainty. For education is nothing if not teaching a skeptical process that exists only in change and exchange. One does not learn what *Moby Dick* "means." One learns how to read and enjoy *Moby Dick* and to engage in the process of reading and enjoying more than *Moby Dick*. To understand and decipher the sometime humor of a big book about whaling. In similar fashion, one does not attend a lecture to write down what is "true" but to engage with ideas, which may involve discussion, which may in turn alter the ideas, which may require additional discussion. If a teacher enters a classroom with notes about what are essentially theories, he is entering the classroom under false pretenses because theories are nothing more than fixed propositions, not manners of engagement (though they could be that); in general, theorists have worked backward from desired conclusions—this is what I want to be true, therefore this is how we get to what I want to be true. Add a dash of obfuscation into the hard shell of icing and you get a birthday "cake" that is inedible.

And it, too, comes without warning unless we listen closely.

THE DEATH OF MR. DARDS

Stanley Dards, who switched out of teaching high school to grammar school because he thought the younger unformed or forming minds might yet have a chance to learn from him, was Clara's favorite instructor. At least he was one among several, given that she has great respect for everyone who labors in the trenches without being remunerated with salary or regard by a nonreading public that feels itself to be nearly complete in education and knowledge, parents who paste on their cars PROUD CAREGIVER OF AN HONORS STUDENT AT SHEEPDIP HIGH (or, in Clara Bean's case, LITETRIP ELEMENTARY SCHOOL, which bumper sticker never made it past the recycle bin between the garage and the rear door to her house).

But Stan Dards died. Run down by a mom in a hurry to run a redding light as he crossed from the faculty parking lot beside the internment camp called "day care" to the concrete walk that slopes gently up to the swing doors of Litetrip School.

The mom was aghast. "What was he doing there? I looked up and there he was, right in front of my car. Just as I hit the 'u' on my keyboard, my car hit him and he flew up and over my Dodge Ram's hood to land in the cargo bay."

"Hard to imagine," other mothers were heard to commiserate.

"He was in the crosswalk," I mentioned, gathering curious looks of question and query as though to ask me what the heck that had to do with it.

The Ram missed the light and thus was forced to stop. Only then did the mother happen to notice that there was a tub of guts in the bed of her truck, a tub of guts known formerly as Stanley Dards, Litetrip School's geometry teacher and coach of girls' field hockey, as well as football practice for boys whose parents thought the continuous bumping of brains against the inside of the biological helmet known as the "head" (they'd learned that in school themselves) would not cause serious injury or mental degradation until long after the parental units were dead and gone at which point they'd have been not caring about their boys for decades.

"Where," demanded one of the more self-righteous survivors of this traumatic event, "was that Mrs. Dunfor?" in a tone that sounded an awful lot to me like calling her a lazy bitch.

Mrs. Dunfor, the language arts teacher, doubled as the morning and after-school crossing guard. Ever since the Black woman who used to hold that job, trundling out into the middle lane with a handheld stop sign blinking with tiny red Xmas lights, was flattened by a color-blind bus driver who claimed he thought the blinking reds were green. In the early gloam of a wintry morning, he did not even see that the blinks were held atop a Black arm like the torch on the Statue of Liberty.

Crossing guard was a dangerous job, second only to waste management workers who daily get crushed by the hydraulics of their back-loading trucks. As such, it provided "danger pay," an extra $5 per morning—per morning, if you can believe that—over the base pay of $12 per morning that Mrs. Dunfor received, for which she was grateful because it kept her off food stamps. After all, when you added in the afternoons, Mrs. Dunfor took in $6,000 extra per school year.

Properly invested, after thirty years when Mrs. Dunfor had become Mrs. Wearier, that $6,000 a year would provide over $700,000 in retirement savings, more than enough after inflation to keep her from needing to abuse the generosity of Republican lawmakers and accept the two boxes of donated food from Kroger or Meijer, which is what they had turned food stamps into. Mrs. Dunfor already having achieved the refined age of 51 meant that she had only to set her alarm or correct the wheelbarrows filled with theme notebooks until she was 81, and given the Cadillac benefits schoolteachers receive (not to mention the long vacations and particular daily down times of "prep" periods scattered like rice throughout their weeks), at 81 she would not be more than 106 in biological age. So it was doable. It was, as my alcoholic aunt used to say, popping the tab on yet another beer, a very easy job.

Of course, there's no accounting for the ways in which Mrs. Dunfor failed to save and invest her windfall earnings but, rather, given her rich salary for doing practically nothing, spent it on wasteful things like heat and electricity. Go figure.

On the morning in question, Mrs. Dunfor, whose shift ended at 8:15, had waited until 8:20 before hurrying inside the school to change hats and become the artless language arts teacher, dividing children into groups to research the meanings of words like "licorice." It didn't take a whole lot of effort to place the attentive girls (three in total) into one separate group, letting the other gaggles of children glom about like bleating lambs as long as they kept their bleating down. Just when Clara Bean was about to question her friend Olivia's pronunciation of "licorice," the office intercom stubbed into the wall behind the Dunfor desk crackled with the news: Stanley Dards was dead. Run down before his prime.

Of the thirty-three kids in the room, only Clara Bean, Olivia, DeVon, and Charlie "don't call me Chuck" seemed to notice. As well as Mrs. Dunfor, whose tired hands fluttered about her eyebrows as she took in the news. She didn't know what to do when a table of girls whose names she would have recognized but couldn't precisely recall began to weep over the fact that field hockey practice might end up canceled that day and that would mean having to cross the street with the troop of poors to the community center's day-care facility to punch in as visitors until their mothers or fathers could sneak into the lot in their polished BMWs and Audi SUVs. These girls wailed at the loss of Stan Dards while secretly hoping and praying that their mothers would remember the hand sanitizer. After three hours of touching furniture or kick balls the poors touched, they'd need it.

But then, after all, they were survivors, a fact that was made plain and was emphasized as the entire population of the school was lined up and walked down to the gymnasium where a woman the size of an office nurse stood on bare legs as thick and sturdy as prairie fence posts in sensible black pumps and mildly called them all "survivors." She explained how the blow to their emotional structures could be permanently damaging if they did not spend time talking to their teachers and counselors and friends about what Mr. Dards had meant to them both individually and collectively. How participating in the grief workshops that would replace attending classes for the remainder of the month was a necessary way for them to pause and find ways in which to reconstruct and establish the binderies of their boundaries, their senses of community.

The cellulite flab quivering as the psychologist lifted her arm and swept the bleachers taking all of them into its horizontal arc, she taught them a chant, "We Are . . . Alive / We Will . . . Survive," a group therapy that pushed the fact and fear of dying away from them, who were too young and vulnerable to have to pay death any attention.

At the end of an hour's chanting, the principal came out to the microphone stand and, while the school's teachers distributed prefabricated white crosses for each of them to take home and decorate and bring back to school if they wished, announced that she would take over girls' field hockey practice and that Mr. Faile had generously offered to run the boys' football practice. Therefore—to the relief of all the children, poor and rich alike—no one need be interfered with because of the untimely death of Stanley Dards, who, she added mysteriously, as though he had a metastasized cancer, had been in reality dying for a long, long time.

GRATITUDE

"What did you do today in Feelings class?"

It used to be "reading, writing, and logic," but then some educationist got the wild hair that reading and requiring reading was injurious to the budding selves that were Clara Bean's classmates. The following year, the educationist's educationist realized that if reading was bad, then so was writing, unless it was about things that mattered to little formatives like their feelings and, given that logic had just rolled wearily over in its dumpster and snuggled down for warmth among the rotten heads of lettuce and eggplant and sighed, got the school board to dispense with such archaic oppressions as reading and writing, and substituted for it all the "rubric" of "Feelings class."

"Discussed," Bean says with a certain disgust. She doesn't enjoy Feelings class. It bores her to dimness.

"Ah," I say. Then, unwilling to leave her in her slough of despond alone, I ask what they discussed. With a feeling that I am being not merely magnanimous but giving because if anything bores me more it's the repeated personal expressions of feeling by the people who need to feel less. This is Bean, after all, who is content to feel and not tell you endlessly about her feelings. "What was the topic?"

I don't laugh at the word "topic," though I know that the truly innovative aspect of Feelings class is that there is no topic. Even if one kid does all the feeling, the topic is amorphous and generally has to do with a sense of victimhood, of pain and the feeling that the world is against the speaker. But as anyone may know, the world is simply the world and there is rarely any for or against to it. Mother Nature does not care about us; if we destroy the planet, we won't destroy the planet but only ourselves; the planet will go on and on and on and Mother Nature will adapt readily, even if all that's left alive are roaches (the skitterish kind) (maybe both, the burnt fag ends of overcome feelings as well as the low black skitterish kind).

We walk in silence, each of us thinking.

"Colleen thinks Mrs. Woofer hates her because she's Irish and has ginger hair."

"And what does Woofer woo . . . say about that?"

"She thinks it's nonsense, I can tell. But she doesn't say that. She says that Colleen's feelings are valid and that given their validity she will try harder to remonstrate how much she likes Colleen and that maybe it's liking her so much that causes her to hold herself back, seem distant and aloof when really all she'd like to do is give Colleen a big hug." Bean walks farther, thinking. "She means demonstrate. Not remonstrate. But she said 'remonstrate.'"

"Words are hard. Sort of like your Artifice teacher." Miss Acrylic says "heart rendering" instead of "heart rending" when she tells a child that her scribbling beyond the shapes and lines framing the images on the page are full of deep emotional expression. "Artifice class"— this continued need to gloss—is formerly "art class" but without the making of art and reduced simply to making. DeVon, I know, is completing a canvas of pallet-knife acrylic colors circled like two bruised eyes, the purpose of which is to "make" you feel sick. A sort of clever double project that will be his term project for both his Artifice and his Feelings classes. Who says he doesn't belong at this school of choice?

"What else did you discuss?"

"How Sue Ellen is a victim."

"Why?"

"She wants a new bike."

"And?"

"Her mom says she can't afford it."

"Ah," I say, buying time. Then, "What's she do?" I ask, figuring Clara knows I mean for a living.

"When?"

"When?"

Clara Bean laughs a crystalline laugh, shiny and bright and with the purest of tones. "She has three jobs," she says, growing serious, her laughter cut off quickly by the serious edge of this information. I know there are women, oftentimes single mothers, who hold down serial jobs in order to buy food, pay heat and rent. Usually those single moms live near major cities, not out here in the Midwest where most cities sing in a minor key and our capital city is more minor than most.

"Sue Ellen feels like her mom's just using that as an excuse. She feels bad, too, sad because other kids get so much more."

Of course, I think. Most kids feel things and one of the things they feel is that they don't get as much as other kids. Bean is not one of these. When Sue Ellen or Ellen Sue or any other kid feels bad, though, Clara tends to feel bad for them. It's empathy, a characteristic most people are losing.

"You remember about Coyote and the Prairie Dogs?"

"Not really." She grins up at me. Even though she does and even though I know she does, her saying "not really" is like her saying "no." It doesn't mean that she doesn't remember. It means that she wants me to tell her again. She wants to hear how the story will change details and events because the stories aren't memorized and told only one way. Stories are told for entertainment and for the purpose of learning—something—and stories told over and over become legends until they are so ingrained in a community's soul that they become myths that tell us how a community is. Leave Freud out of it and the Oedipus myth becomes a story as much about fatedness where three roads cross, as well as a pre-Christian recognition of the role the number three plays in myths and legends and stories. Consider: it's not just the Father, Son, and Holy Ghost but also Jesus, Joseph, and Mary. Threes are big: it could be a girl, her fiancé, and a group of invisible Japanese Gentlemen (treated, narratively, as one and not eight individual persons) in Graham Greene's "The Invisible Japanese Gentlemen." Threes are good: a hero or protagonist in concert or conflict with two other characters, one secondary, the other tertiary to reflect and reveal things about either of the first two in context. Without the reflectors or ficelles, a listener or reader realizes only that a solitary, isolated character is as nothing; a hero or heroine reveals little or nothing without other characters in a context. Thus, the isolated meditative figure completely alone on a mountain top feeling victimized but unsure by whom is not alive in the true sense of the word because he is not in context, conflict, or agreement with other human beings. He may as well be a holy ghost, for all that.

"So Coyote was out on the prairie just going along and going along like he does, feeling kind of lonely and in need of someone to talk with, at, or to, when he came upon a field of dirt volcanoes, which were the entrances and exits to the underground safety of a community of prairie dogs. Outside of one volcano stood a prairie dog, ramrod straight, turning his head this way and that and ready to dive underground if Coyote made one wrong move.

"'Hey,' Coyote said.

"'Hey, hey,' said the Prairie Dog, whose name was Martin.

"'What's up, dog?'

"'Martin flinched at the immediate informality of 'dog.' It made him wary of the wolf in gray Coyote's fur. To avoid being impolite, however, he answered, 'Me. I. I am up, as you can see.' He stretched his back, rising to his full height. Keeping one eye cocked on Coyote, ready to dive into the volcano top of one of the burrows, he surveyed the plains. A shadow floated across the dirt. High up, a chicken hawk circled lazily on the breeze that he couldn't feel on the surface of the earth though he did see a tumbleweed trying to start a tumble, pulling its thorns free of the earth.

"'Hah, I meant what's happening?'

"'Not much, as you can see.' Although he hated to bring up food and eating when faced with someone like Coyote who might himself be hungry, Martin felt the need to qualify the 'much.'

"'It's lunchtime,' Martin said. 'Everyone's indoors eating nuts and grass. Just about finished. Then it'll be naptime for the little ones.'

"'You got pine nuts?' Coyote came from the Rockies, and his favorite foods were pine nuts and salmon.

"'Nah. Raw peanuts, mostly. A few acorns.'

"'Those dogs way over beyond there got pine nuts. Want me to go borrow you some?'

"'Nah. We have enough.'

"'Without pine nuts, your fur gets all itchy and mottled.'

"'True. Still, we have fingernails to scratch with.'

"'Their fur is shiny. Smooth.'

"'Great.'

"'You don't want shiny fur?'

"'Sure. We'd like that. But as I said, we're good.'

"'Right.' Coyote thought. 'They've got stones, too. Quartz. They're using the quartz to make a dam. Put a river between you and them.'

"Martin shrugged. 'Water is good. It'll help us, too. They're good neighbors. We're lucky to have such good neighbors. There, but they leave us alone except if we need them.'

"He seemed to feel lucky to be alive and grateful to be able to forage and cavort on the Great Plains. Coyote, with his usual meddling to make the world anew, asked Martin why he didn't mind that the other dogs seemed to have more things like stones with quartz that caught the evening sun and made it pink, to which he replied, 'Can't say, really. But we don't.'

"'What they have you don't and won't,' Coyote howled.

"'Live and let live,' he told Coyote Old Man. 'We'll knit them sweaters when the spring rains come. Ship them over and feel real good. About ourselves.'

"Not knowing what else to say or to do, Coyote hung around scratching himself.

"That night, Martin began to think, wandering wondering around his den while his children dined again on some of the grasses stored up in a clutch of rock by Mrs. Martin. And you know what can happen when Prairie Dogs start to think too much."

Bean nodded. For now she was enjoying the story.

"The next day, Old Man was back again, loping over from away and jumping the new stream, which was really a strand of connected ponds. He began to hang about the entrance to Martin's burrow, whispering to

Mrs. Martin and the little ones about the things they lacked, sneering and pointing out many of the things the other band of dogs had and asking if they didn't think that life on the prairie ought to be more fair.

"'New fur,' he whispered. 'Shiny coat. Warmer than the ones you got.'

"'Go away,' Mrs. Martin said to Old Man when her youngest became teary over the fact that he lacked a shelf of his own to sleep on. 'Get your snout out of our burrow. Please,' she added, not wishing to be excessively rude and offend Coyote.

"'Don't worry, I won't hurt you,' Coyote replied, thinking that she might be afraid for her little ones.

"But Mrs. Martin was smart. Wise. 'Unless it hurts to be eaten,' she said. 'Now go.' And she scurried across the den with a paddle and blumped Coyote on his snout."

Bean says, "That was a mistake."

"Sure was," I reply, proud that she's already ahead of me. "That gave Old Man purpose. For weeks, he showed up at the entrance to the burrow and spent his lazy days whispering about how these Prairie Dogs worked hard and got only peanuts while their fur grew mottled and patchy, rubbed away as they lived what he called a hardscrabble life.

"'Look at what you don't have,' he told them.

"'We have enough,' they said back.

"'More than enough,' others said, calmly going about filling their storerooms with a surfeit of nuts, thankful for all they had."

Bean casts me one of her moon-faced knowing looks. She knows that one of my favorite anecdotes to tell my students is the one about Norman Mailer at a cocktail party listening to a hedge-fund manager go on and on about how much he earned last year and asking Norman if he doesn't wish he had more. "I have one thing you'll never have," Mailer replies. The fund manager splutters in disbelief and demands to know what, at which point Mailer simply smiles, sips his drink, and then replies, "Enough." I tell the anecdote at semester's end as I wish—and I really do—them all to have enough as they leave our class together.

I continue:

"But Coyote persisted. He turned to the kids. 'Look what you don't have,' he told the younger ones. If they sounded like their parents and said they had enough, he simply sneered and pointed out all the Prairie Dogs around them who had more. He told them it wasn't fair, and he told them it wasn't fair in a tone that sounded true as though life on the prairie plains ought to be fair. That indeed there was a thing called fairness that was more than justice, which was fair. Over and over he told them these things.

"Before long, the three kids began to feel like victims because other Prairie Dogs had more bikes or balls to play with, dolls, or Legos to spread out on the floor and build with when it rained and they couldn't go outside for fear of being washed away.

"The little Martins began to feel and what they felt was first that they didn't have things. Then they felt that the things they did have weren't enough. Then they felt that their parents were just making this enough stuff up to keep them in line and so they decided to go out and find things out for themselves without their parents knowing.

"On the Night of the New Moon, they waited until everything was as dark as pitch and their parents were snoring, tucked up on their queen-size shelf. Then they climbed down silently and sneaked across the burrow to climb one by one up and out of the volcano and began to creep across the prairie toward the other village of Prairie Dogs. Suddenly, a beat of wings like Leda being taken by the Swan, and an Owl took off the smallest of the Martins. Stumbling into one of the stream ponds, the next biggest caught his foot beneath a stone that rolled over on him and caused him to lose his footing and drown. The biggest, feeling rather proud of herself and superior to her weakling brother and sister, crossed the pond and managed to climb out only to run into an open snout beneath two glowing Coyote eyes. Though it wasn't a lot to eat, she was enough for a goodly snack for Old Man, who loped off toward home shaking his head at the way his whispering had worked on the Martin children.

"And that was how Martin and Mrs. Martin came to have more food than they needed. But," I say, holding up my forefinger as Bean's mouth opens to speak, "but without their kids they never again had enough."

Bean gives me a wistful smile as we turn the corner toward home, knowing that what Bumpa has just told her is that she is more than enough now and for always, regardless of what other old dogs may have.

GRADING MILLENNIALS

C lara's "uncs" sent me a link. "Too much for Nugget, you think?"
Nugget is his nickname for Clara Bean. The joy she carries
into the room you're in makes you want to give her a special name that only you share with her. She collects nicknames like
sidewalk chalk. So far, Clara has Cloobie, Bean, Beaner, and Nugget.
Cloobie is a family matter, the daughter of Moobie and Roobie.

Uncs had sent me a link to YouTube, a song about Millennials, titled,
with all the appropriateness of contemporary song titling, "You've
Gotta Love Millennials." The song is witty. It's satire, poking fun at
young people who believe they'll not only be but also will deserve to
be millionaires by thirty without doing any work, at girls posting sel-
fies with inspirational quotations as though these describe the girls'
wisdom, and at the idea that Millennials don't take criticism well at all
(just look at the blowback Millennials have given the song). It makes a
professor who teaches Millennials laugh. It's meant to make you laugh.
And, like all satire, not a little at yourself, regardless of your age. But
like venal proposals in Congress that also must be meant to make you
laugh, they soon lose their humorousness, their humorarity. Thinking people know that the greediest and worst of congressmen aren't
joking, though they themselves are laughing all the way to the bank.
Teachers—and others who work with Millennials, like the police—find
the wit true; sad, but true. They have tried and failed to get Millennials to
focus long enough to learn to read.

Millennials themselves look out from their photo albums of self-
ies long enough to recognize that the song is about them. Like poor
Whites in the South who have been falling for the evangelical magic of
tax cuts that privilege the wealthy while keeping the unwealthy realis-
tically restricted—"We'll cut everyone's tab 10 percent, leaving you an
extra hundred and fifty dollars per year to spend as you want, not the

lib'ral guberment that would've paved your roads or provided basic health care"—they feel very like awesomely angry and mill around voting booths like tattoo parlors.

The Millennial song would be endlessly funny if it weren't true. Lines about getting a trophy "just for participating" is merely one of the problems.

Educationists who invented inclusive trophy-getting meant well. I'll grant you that. But only grudgingly because a large part of my thinking suggests that they meant little other than to protect their jobs by shifting the social ground beneath the public's feet. When you don't do anything worthwhile for a living, you spend your days attending long meetings trying to find ways to justify the nothingness, and educationists hit on a kind of protected inclusivity that seats the capable right next to the incapable, the willing-to-learn beside the dopamined cul-de-sacs of skulls.

I mean, you don't want little LeCant getting her feelings hurt for living up to her name; you want her to have a positive outlook and hope for a future more meaningful than the logo stenciled on her T-shirt. How do you do that if you don't want to fail her and still prod her (gently and without touching her person) to help her work harder to learn something? You give it to her. You create the good feeling by giving her a trophy for the mash of clay she's fired into a . . . well . . . shape. You keep up with the trophies, giving her another when she drops jars of paint onto paper and hangs the slough of postmodern art on the cinder-block walls of the hallway (otherwise known as the "Gallery" on Parents' Night).

In case her parents notice how awful her clay works and painting are, you give them a bumper sticker for their car that reads, I HAVE AN HONOR ROLL STUDENT AT X SCHOOL so they can drive little LeCant homeward, everyone feeling good as they announce to the world what the middle class does not know: everyone is on the honor roll and everyone gets a certificate for attendance at year end; as long as they showed up on 70 percent of the reduced number of school days (budgets being tight with taxes so low), they are guaranteed to pass along into the next grade of cautious torpor.

As the comic Bill Burr says: Seven out of ten, Flossie. Seven out of ten.

Except nowadays it's 9.5 out of 10. Students who receive less than a B+ complain, often to the people required to hear their complaints, associate department chairs and counselors.

"How do you know that?" Beaner asks.

"Let me tell you a story."

Whereas most of my family immediately discover things that they have to do when I say something like "Let me tell you a story," Beaner has time.

"Once upon a time," I begin, "there were three Squirrels named Zoë, Muerte, and Pendejo."

"I thought you said all Squirrels were named Stuart or Frankie."

"I did. But those are our Squirrels. They are special. They're the ones gamboling and cavorting and flicking their squirrely hellos when we stroll past in the evenings. Besides, that's another story."

"Ah."

"So anyway," I begin again, recognizing that though grammatically okay, I've just used the "so" construction that has permeated interviewees and news reporters: "How has al-Assad committed war crimes?" "So, he . . ." Or "What's the weather going to be like?" "So today it will be . . ." (with the certainty of forecasting anything future, which in Michigan is somewhat like England—"Don't like the weather? Just wait a minute"). It's annoying enough to have someone tell you that the wet stuff that soaked your jacket was, lo and behold, rain, heavy at times (as when you were dashing to your car), without having every freaking response begin with "So" with as much meaning as "fa-so-la-ti-do."

"Anyway, one day Zoë, Muerte, and Pendejo came home with the results of year-end tests that measure nothing more than a Squirrel's ability to take tests. Muerte had gotten a zero, as Muerte ought. Pendejo had gotten a 2.5 for having the aspirational interest to cheat, though off the answer sheets of the wrong student. Zoë had gotten a 5 out of 10. Average, as so much of Zoë is.

"Mrs. Mutter, needless to say, was not pleased. She knew, well, she *felt*, that there must be some mistake. Her three children had always been exceptional.

"'Au contraire,' Mrs. Dards told her when Mrs. Mutter helicoptered her way into school to meet with her.

"Wean Dards ('Call me Wean'), the widow of Stan Dards, was Pendejo's teacher for high-school Attendance class where Pendejo, who was lost much of the time, managed to find the classroom only about 40 percent of the time. Thus, a less-than-perfect grade. (Mrs. Dards, like all teachers, was not allowed to use the word 'fail.' And thus, years later, when the airplane's wing broke off the plane that Pendejo helped manufacture, the wing did not 'fail' but was only less than supportive.)

"Dards was sorry, she told Mutter, but there was little she could do about it unless she wanted to purchase a handheld GPS for little lost Pendejo so he could find his class in interventions that he was required to take and at the end of which he would receive—if he attended at least 80 percent of the time—his Honors Certificate for Attendance and Sensitivity to Issues, and all would be well once again in the Mutter household.

"Mutter recognized a victimizer when she saw one. Yet she did admit that living with Pendejo was kind of hairy. She martialed her feelings and turned to her middling child, Muerte, encouraging her with all sympathy to file a grievance against the professor who gave her a zero as though Muerte did not matter.

"Muerte being a constant and determined girl, always hanging around to surprise people when they least expected her, did as instructed. She went to the grievance hearing where—with the professor out of the room so she'd not feel intimidated and victimized more than she was already—she carefully explained that she felt she should pass the course because, after all, she had bought the books.

"The associate dean, witless in the face of Muerte's nontraditional illegal counselor, decided that she had a point. When the professor was invited to reenter the room from his detention in the hallway out-side, the dean informed him that he was changing Muerte's grade to a 'pass,' retroactively enrolling her in the lecture course on a 'pass/not pass' basis.

"El professor, being savvy if not intelligent, understood the hierar-chy of power (not wit) in the educational institution. He controlled his anger and went back to his office and immediately altered 149 grades in the 1-to-4 spectrum (zeroes were reserved only for no-shows like the student who had just passed, because otherwise a professor is oppress-ing a student who is, in all respects but intelligence and knowledge, deeply felt to be the professor's equal) to 4.0s. As."

"As in Oakland?" Beaner inquires. Her father is a huge baseball fan.

"As in Anywhere, US of A."

We were nearly at the park. Bean began to skip with expectation. "What happened to Zoë, Bumpa?"

"She came to my office, I mean the professor's office, to say that there must be some mistake."

"She wanted a higher grade?"

The logical extension of Bean's idea was attractive. Why not change the 4-point grading scale to an 8-point one without telling stu-dents? Then they would get closer to their rightful grades. But that would never fly, like most of my ideas. After all, the Education Depart-ment would then be required to invent yet another rubric—a term they like a lot to show how grades were going to be assigned or, rather, not "Assigned" but "Given" or, perhaps, "Gifted."

"No. She wanted the grade she should have gotten. A five out of ten. After all, she said, life is rarely better than above average, regardless of the number of trophies one collects while living it."

"What did this professor do?"

"I gave her a trophy."

4

Not Nobody

NOT NOBODY

This is "Be All that You Can Be" week in Clara Bean's school, and some fool from the local university's Education Department spent the afternoon telling Beaner's class that they could be all that they wanted to be, an adaptation of the US Army's "Be all that you can be." To inculcate this idea into the little vats of bone and blood sitting cross-legged on the gymnasium floor, they chanted "You are somebody" over and over and in between.

Being what one wants to be is not the same as being all that one can be. The slogans not only involve the differences between "can" and "want" but—in the case of the army—also involve taking long and honest looks at the basic material out of which the "can" may be made.

"Ms. Fickele said we can be anything we want in the modern world now today."

I can feel the waiting tension in Bean's grip, the way she knows how much I object to verbal constructions that try to use here and now–ness to gain the veneer of importance while denying the old-hattedness of what once, as distant as last year, were good ideas, which may have developed over years, even centuries, gone by. Bean knows that I think that human beings have changed little since the hairy dawn of *2001: A Space Odyssey*. They certainly still do the same things, like love or hook up, fight and argue, disagree and agree and, with careful thinking and possibly education, grow less intolerant, and no matter how much money Big Pharma invests, they still grow old and die.

"Ms. Fickele says we should want to be somebody, to be important, and to change the world."

"What does Mrs. Weary say?"

"Nothing."

Wise choice, I think.

"She made us all say what it was we wanted to be."

"Did you say anything?"

She shrugged. Shook her head. No. She hadn't. She'd learned the lesson of Odysseus, that shouting out your name and origins can wreak havoc on your travel plans. At first, that man known as a master storyteller told the one-eyed monster Polyphemous that his name was "Nobody," and Polyphemous, enamored of the importance of names and branding, went around laughing at Nobody while eating Odysseus's men two by two. Clever to the end, Odysseus heats a sharpened log and, when the Cyclops is sleeping, rams it home in his eye, blinding him. Even more clever is the way he and his last six crew men hang below the fleecy bellies of the Cyclops's fattened sheep, and when the monster rolls aside the massive stone to allow the sheep out to graze the next day, they are free to run to their ship and row out beyond the grasp of the Cyclops, where, in a moment of hubris, Odysseus shouts back at the monster that his name is not Nobody but Odysseus, son of Laertes, from Ithaka, getting for his proud foolhardiness a massive boulder thrown at him by Polyphemous, barely missing his ship. Worse. Going from Nobody to Somebody allows Polyphemous to protest to Dad about his blinding, and Dad just happens to be Poseidon, who, though he cannot keep Odysseus from Ithaka and home because Athena protects her favorite hero, can and does throw storms and tempests at Odysseus, wrecking his ship and killing his crew, leaving the Greek hero alone to float to the shores of an unknown island, doubling Odysseus's pride-filled homecoming journey to twenty years.

It is this dangerous shift from Nobody to Somebody that the writer William Kennedy talks about. After years of rejection (who wants to read a novel about bums in Albany?), getting blank looks from inquisitors who wanted to know what he had published—not written but published for the grand sums all writers who matter get—in his speech accepting a major prize in literature, Kennedy described himself as "Not Nobody." It's important to note Kennedy's wisdom and perspicuity. The movement from Nobody to Not Nobody is not the same as the movement from Nobody to Somebody. A sudden leap from Nobody to Somebody is a jump into a chasm that is dark with narcissism and self-regard and demands, even to the extreme of corruption, sycophancy, and an almost psychopathic childishness, the trumpeting of one's name and the misty fog blurring his lack of accomplishment.

It leaves a writer (as well as a person) who previously learned balance and philosophy and humility stunned by imbalance and egotism. Timing is everything—and the timing is individually relative. If it's Bean in early schooling and she gets told chantingly, "You are somebody," and she believes it (and she doesn't have a bumpa to qualify that believing), there may be trouble. Sure, she is somebody to Bumpa, to her family; to her teachers, she is definitely not nobody, though; to the white Audi that runs her over as she inattentively crosses the street, she is nobody, still, until the police or ambulance men arrive to record her as somebody the texting driver of the Audi ought to have paid attention to. It is that that I teach her: how someone so endlessly important to Bumpa might be endingly unimportant to an inattentive driver or how apparently unimportant Arleigh is to Mrs. Arleigh when she runs out of school to tell her all about her day and Mrs. Arleigh is too busy surfing the internet on her phone to listen or care.

Is that too easy? Well, how about a young writer? How many creative writing students in college, still believing the chant that they are somebody, want not criticism (that's for apprentice writers, not talents like themselves) but praise? How many assume it's simply a matter of putting words—words unheard or imprecise or shallow—on the page, being recognized as a "talent" by an editor willing to advance unseemly amounts of money, and then going on tour to sign autographs for the lines of adoring fans?

First of all, putting words on a page (or on a computer terminal's screen) is easy. But what happens when you reread those words? Are they spelled correctly? Are your discrete ideas discreet? Does your main character drink drafty beer and for his troubles gain little more than a belch of air? Have you stayed staid, or are you obsessed with wokeness and stile? Or should you "have went" to class at all? Is the project of your story "heart rendering" as a student once wrote, tearing tearfully the tare wait of the burden all students bare with their agendas? That's all *sic*.

I used to require students to read their writing aloud, recommending that they take time out from being woke to read it aloud to themselves at home before wasting the paper to print it, which few ever did. One could tell they had not, listening to them falter as their sentences became unwieldy and confused and their brains began to short-circuit, their voices falling, their rhythm failing, their words turning into the colorless all-color of Melville's White Whale and needing a gold doubloon nailed to their foreheads to give them significance or meaning or even the pleasurable processes of hearing a well-turned phrase or perception or pun until, out of pity and a desire to alleviate what had to be their humiliation, I would say, "That's enough," and watch them grow angry, having been unaware—of so many things but, in this case, specifically of their idiocy, of how stupid they sounded and how bored their colleagues were as they tried to pay attention and listen while thinking about their own writing and how much better it would be than this, to which, when the end was ended and the questions questioned—"What do you think?"—they would inevitably answer "I liked it" in an attempt to establish a baseline for liking that was so low that no matter what people really thought, they would be forced to (1) respond in kind, or (2) even if they didn't (like it, that is), they would dislike theirs a whole lot less than this one and their saying that they liked it would be a whole lot more sincere, more honest, and in this way everyone in the class would feel as though he or she had gotten a prize, a blue ribbon that said, *Gee, Biscayne, you actually got out of bed and wrote words. Good for you. I especially like the extra exclamation marks you put near the ends of your seeming sentences. They lend so much more meaning and the emphasis is nearly overwhelming.*

Second, even if the editor is sort of right (please forgive my diplomatic imprecision), and she detects in the miasma of your writing some skill and possible future promise, which she calls "talent," is she really referring to talent? Or simply to some notion that this stuff might sell?

Talent, which derives from "balance" or "a sum of money," is not aptitude or skill but a means of exchange and, as such, requires at least two people, a buyer and a seller, a reader and a writer, a giver and a taker—though remembering the part of talent that is "balance," the taking is more of an accepting and not a getting. Thus Faulkner, who is arguably the writing genius of the American twentieth century, needed his editor to edit, to bring The Sound into balance with The Fury. I agree with Macbeth that "life struts and frets his hour . . . a tale told by an idiot." Or can be. But I don't agree that all life signifies nothing.

Maybe it's the Indian in me, Bean, but all the love we've exchanged is not nothing, and I think life is the presence or absence of love. Apart from that, in conjunction with William Kennedy's wisdom and humor about becoming Not Nobody, it raises questions: Does one want—truly want—to be Somebody?

Do we ever ask children to gradually expand their horizons and think not "I want to be this or that" but ask "Do I truly want to be this or that with all the attendant notoriety that goes with the being?" In an age in which notability—people recognizing your name because of the successful processes in which you have engaged (from preventing a child from being hurt, perhaps, to rescuing your combat compatriots in a war that should never have been begun, or writing an engaging book that is worth reading or leading a movement against racism or homophobia, or, at sixteen, sailing on a solar-powered boat from Sweden to the United States to deliver a scathing, true, and impassioned and moving speech about climate change at the United Nations)—seems to struggle against rising notoriety (shamelessly breaking federal and state laws, mistreating immigrants or women or Epstein girls, fostering hatred, childishness, division, venality and cowardice and selfishness in the extreme), we fail to stop and contextualize our thinking.

If Bean wants to be a dancer—and what middle-class little girl whose family loves and participates in art and music and philosophy hasn't at one point imagined herself as "dancer dancing" in tutu and slippers, soaring in grace and beauty, lifted and held by Russian men in tights, enacting the role of Odile—she may take dance lessons (as long as the lessons do not involve the crippling of going en pointe) or go to the ballet with Nana. But no one ought to be fooled: she most likely cannot be what she momentarily dreams of being; but she can and may develop a sense of line and movement, a dancing way of relating a narrative.

Just as a painting class or two might help her understand what Bumpa understood half a century ago, which was that there is Rembrandt, Vermeer, Bruegel, Kandinsky, Matisse—always Matisse—and there was himself. Polar opposites in significance and beauty. Although in being all that I can be I will never be a great or even a good painter (I lack sufficient inclination for the training and effort that would be required), one day I want to take Clara Bean to Florence and let her stand in that room in the Uffizi Gallery with a young, middle-aged, and elderly Rembrandt self-portrait and allow her to see, in the colors and brushstroke textures and sheer unadulterated talent of the painter, the changes and feelings and attitudes that age brings to a perceiving life because while I—and I doubt very many other human beings—could never be or have been Rembrandt or painted anything as wonderful and moving as those, to see them lifts the heart and codifies the mindfulness of life and if there is a soul enriches it.

It is the same enrichment, the same calm, broadly felt pleasure that comes from having your wife hand you Graham Swift's *Waterland* and asking you what you thought. Reading the first few pages, standing there in the bookstore in Brooklyn, and after fifty years of writing yourself, you reply, "I don't know. But he knows what he is doing," encouraging her to buy it, read it, let you read it. The joy that comes from that novel is overwhelming. It is so well told, so plain and apparently simple and so good, as good as Elizabeth Bowens's *The Death of the Heart*, great, even—although the word "great" is almost useless when you have Homer, or Dante, or *Njal's Saga* and *The Tale of Genji*,

Amos Tutuola, Ernest Gaines, or Pär Lagervist's *The Dwarf* among a thousand other writers who occupy a height overlooking, shading, or encapsulating the soul of the world, telling us who we are and how we might want to be being.

They are all notable and deserving our notice. But so is the human being who lives on a human being's scale. Bean may become a solar panel installer or an editor or agent (each of whom helps us be who we are in better ways). Maybe a doctor, a lawyer, the head of a nonprofit for the rights of women and men, veterans, families separated at the border (whether the Latino families of today or the descendants of African families where fathers were sold away from wives and children, children were sold away from their mothers or grandparents, in our history of racism and cruelty).

The scale we choose should, with some foresight and parental or teacherly guidance, match the circumference of our happiness. I once received more than four thousand death threats for saying in front of a lecture class, "Remember: If you want to be Mitt Romney, you have to *be* Mitt Romney." I might as easily have said Barack Obama (or, for the feminists out there, my son's main crush, Michelle Obama) or John McCain (no one on this planet could really want to be Sarah Palin, standing staring at Russia from her backyard). Or I might have said Midas and risked losing my audience of Millennials who think Midas is a muffler repair shop. Regardless of the name I chose (and Mitt Romney is an honest man, as far as I can tell), the truth remains. If you want to run for president, if you want to represent your state in Congress, you have to do that and do it to the best of your abilities, work hard to learn and grow and offer beneficial governance and possible change.

T. S. Eliot says that no poet or writer has his complete meaning alone. Precisely, Bean. We might extend that: No person has her complete meaning alone. We are Human Beings, and Human Beings we must live with and around; they have to have the chance, at least, to love other Human Beings. A tribe is not a tribe without men, women, and children who belong and who willingly and thoughtfully follow a leader, a "chief." A community is not a community, a state not a state, without communers and staters. And everyone who reads and learns knows that a house divided against itself is not a good thing when Poseidon's hurricanes of change enact their wraths.

The Buddhist monk who separates from social contact and goes to meditate alone needs to dine with other monks. The elementary-school girl who splits off from her cohort and stares alone at the wall feeling whatever a grammar-school girl might feel also needs lunch, preferably a nutritious and balanced one. The politician needs to know history, the law, and tradition and take his or her place in the tradition of service to the nation and not to himself. The teacher needs students to guide, to help learn, and to learn from. The autoworker, the cashier at Whole Foods—the doctor, lawyer, and Indian chiefs—all need others and all need to recognize that they choose to do what they do. It is all there in Sartre's ideas of freedom and responsibility. It is all there in Ernest Gaines's novels, and William Melvin Kelley's, and Evan Connell Jr.'s, none of whom shout out their names or origins to the one-eyed monster of commerce that would devour them with the pressure to write another book just like the last one or consume their time and energy with the attempt to publicly brand their names. None of them is a celebrity, a Somebody whose name is, for good or for ill, recognized by hundreds or thousands or millions of people. Each of them is Not Nobody, though. Each of them contributes to the project that is humanity (even the homeless man on the corner contributes by enlarging our capacities for sympathy, empathy, and generosity).

Mr. Ramsay might stand in the bow of the boat shouting, "We perished, each alone," and he'd be right if we understand that without other people being Human Beings we do, in essence, perish. But he'd be wrong if we understood the process as binary, as either/or, for we live with, for, and because of Human Beings. If we love, we love and probably (but not necessarily or conditionally) feel loved ourselves. If we do, then we never perish. We are joined to (at least) seven generations past and seven generations future. If you are deeply loved, then your seventh great-grandchild will hear you spoken well of, and you will be, in a Native sense, immortal; people (the *Human Beings*) still speak

well of Chief Joseph, and I suspect they will always speak well of him.
But remember, he did not seek to be spoken of at all; he was chosen by
a moment and given who he already was being, he allowed himself to
become Somebody until the end of his life when he sat lonely beside
the nighttime campfire and thought, and what he thought contained a
feeling of regret as well as a feeling of acceptance of the role a man like
him was chosen—by history because of the time, by his people because
of who he was and how well he spoke—to play.

The regret would have been there even if he had not been Somebody. So also would be there the reflection that he had spoken as
truly and well, had lived as Human Being–ly as possible, and he could
never regret that. Christians have a metaphor for the end of life, with
the dying person's life "passing before his eyes" before his shelf life
reaches expiration. Christians seem to find an ending, a completion in
this metaphor—it passes before one's eyes and one judges it (perhaps this is where their god enters to offer the disinterest of judgment)
and breathes his last. But there is no ending, there. Standing around
his deathbed are daughters and granddaughters, sons and grandsons,
wives or partners, and they (while like or antithetically unlike) will
speak well of him or not. Maybe he didn't feel shame when he should
have, or maybe he substituted pride when a process merited only satisfaction. Maybe, in his own small way, he succeeded in being a better
father than his own father, and for that he will be remembered in both
word and deed, tale and anecdote. If he tried hard but did not, perhaps, fully succeed, at least he will have managed to be Not Nobody.
If he doesn't try and remains a bad father then, he will immediately,
upon expiration, begin to be forgotten, and seven generations from the
moment of dying, the forgetting will be certain and complete.

Being spoken well of is what you ought to seek to earn humbly by
being. If you are made to be Somebody, then accept the burden. But
for heaven's sake, don't shout out your name to the monstrous Polyphemous, with his abundance of stories and legends.

In the context of whatever set of processes you choose to involve
yourself—being Not Nobody is what I would have you be, Bean, what,

in the context of the love you share with me and us, you already are. Hearing you, standing at the front door beside your infant brother, at 7:10 a.m., shout to your departing father, "Bye, Daddy, I love you," not only gives me great joy, but it also means in my own Not Nobody way that I've succeeded in something.

It's Ironic

"**W**hy me?" I wrote Bean's uncle (who parades around in the guise of my beloved son). "Why send it to me? Why not ask her parents? I'm Bumpa. I no longer have to make these difficult decisions. I get to slump in an easy chair and drool when I'm not going on about something no one is listening to."

He'd sent me an article about surface. About how the irony of the Platonic dialogues derives from the comic origin of the Eiron, the clever underdog who triumphs repeatedly over the boastful character Alazon, but now the shallow, surface populism of the internet has inverted it so the boastful Alazon repeatedly suppresses the Eiron who is no longer clever but willingly suspicious of skepticism, turning the comic into the tragic. The pervasive infection of irony is the result of thoughtless people taking refuge in screens, and the ease of that damages people of all ages, especially children and those who in their weak logic and skepticism have been left with the minds of children.

The question, the problem at Uncle's hand, was—wanting Bean never to resemble a Millennial—should he and I restrict our satirizing of Millennials and not make them amusing, a symbol-less group of meaningless signs. If we make something funny, satirize it, you want to recognize the commonality it retains with those of us who find it funny. For the shrinking brains out there, we make it entertaining, appealing, with the hope of expanding their perspectives—and there is nothing that entertainment can't make appealing, except perhaps Alec Baldwin's Donald Trump.

I recognized how vulnerable I was at the moment the link showed up in italicized blue. Having just turned in my semester's grades for my classes, I was trapped between the knowledge of what the grades ought to have been and what I gave them. Young people who have been indoctrinated with the idea that they are all special, and effortlessly so, assume that they all will be entrepreneurial millionaires by thirty, or if they really must work, then it will be as doctors dispensing the benefits of Big Pharma for a barely adequate salary. Give students a B grade, which ought to have been a C or lower, and they file grievances and complaints that then take up your time. As someone who is willing to drive a quarter mile out of his way to avoid difficult left turns, circling around a goal via right turns, I am willing to avoid danger and complication (or lazily substitute personal, legal ease for difficulty), but I am not willing to let someone sit in my office asking over and over why he or she is getting a grade that will prevent a career in astrophysics or medical research or simply just the plasticized hair of local newscaster, unwilling to understand—no matter how many turns the conversation has to take—that the measure of performance is not completely subjective, that history, experience, comparison, and even attendance and thoughtful participation play a role in the measure and that I have already given them the highest grade that I could morally and intellectually justify.

I always have told students that they were welcome to complain to me about their grades as long as they accepted the fact that in revisiting the process I might actually lower it to what it should have been. When I tell that to students now, they whine to the associate chair about "microaggressions," as though any measure or standard applied to them is an infringement upon their personal rights. All heterosexual or LGBTQ people deserved high honors for which their parents—who may or may not remember their children's names—are duly proud. Just look at all the stickers on the backs of minivans and SUVs that declare that the person driving distractedly in front of you is a proud parent of an honor student at x high school, middle school, grammar school, preschool, or hospital nursery.

"Pride goeth before a raise," I said to Bean.

She squinched up her face and did her "back back walk," a child's imitation of the singer formerly alive and known as Michael Jackson who succumbed to the promises of Big Pharma. Coming over to give me a hug, laying her head on my bony old knee, she asked, "Now what do you do, Bumpa?"

"Now I give them As. At the worst, B pluses. Otherwise I'd hurt their chances of getting accepted into a medical school in Panama."

"Pana-what?"

"It's a country that specializes in abetting certification for all manner of ills as well as hiding rich people's money."

I do not mention the irony that Panama's Canal Zone is a large district America stole from Columbia, literally stole, in order to cut and build a seawater canal between the Pacific and Atlantic Oceans. Nor do I point out that with the same endemic racism we continue to demonstrate in the United States, using unarmed Black boys as moving targets for police ballistics practice or calling White nationalist racists "good people" in Charlottesville, Virginia, the Black Caribbean laborers who came to the Canal Zone were allowed to live in metal-roofed shanties in the jungle's malarial tangle outside the cities of clean and plumbed housing built for the White workers. Nor do I mention the science deniers back in 1903 who refused even to consider that malaria was mosquito borne and transmitted, not unlike the foolish unread man in tighty-whities who thinks "global warming" and "climate change" are two different and separately unrelated events.

"Where?"

I recognized her attempt to distract me. But I am like a terrier when it comes to education or the lack of it. Plato didn't follow Socrates around sycophantishly begging for a higher mark. It may be wrong—I often am wrong—but grades did not matter then, and I did not and do not care about them now. I figure that a student who gets a B+ either may or may not succeed at doing whatever he wants to do. No doubt, he fantasizes his future life. As Bean already knows, if the expectation of future comes from the awareness and knowledge of a past, these kids have no real expectations but only dreams, which are actually fantasies. Futures to believe in until they can't.

Bean had a future as a reader and a listener because of her past, because of the joy of the wonderful children's books that she heard with an engaged listening that bound her to her reader with whom she shared the pleasure, if not the repetition ad nauseam. Even that endurance, unrevealed, created roots and ties. It obviously created and increased her ability to focus, once she could sit all the way through a story without wriggling to the floor and beginning a Scottish Highland dance.

She likes dancing, and her balletic-bowing exit off the imagined stage resembles her mother's at the same age with genetic determination. By now, Bean has danced the lead role of almost every major ballet available on DVD, Odile being a favorite, along with *The Firebird*'s princess.

"Did you know that a student can file a formal grievance against you for failing her because, having never attended lectures except for exams and having failed all exams, she bought the books?"

It was true. Years ago, a girl grieved against me and my teaching assistant, claiming that purchasing the books for the class entitled her to a passing grade at the very least. I refused to give her one. So the dean called me and asked that if they changed her enrollment to pass/not pass, would I change the grade to a pass. No, I said. I will not. Though you may do anything you want. You are the dean, after all. He took me at my word and also took the opportunity to make her go away. She passed.

"So grades don't matter?"

"It's like life. What matters is that you do your best. It's best if you learn something while doing it."

Now I have a good friend, emeritus now, who spent his career giving out real and honestly earned grades for performance in his college classes, who disapproved mightily of my indifference to grades. But I have two justifications, and perhaps one of them matters.

The first is that the college subject I teach should either not be taught or it ought to be modified radically: creative writing.

Accepting the proposition that all young people with demi-digitized minds have "creativity," even given their passively sitting in front of sitcoms or watching YouTube on their handheld screens for twenty years along with their excessive self-love and senses of self-importance, and combining that with our liberal assumptions that all human beings have some form of fallacious creativity simply by fact of being—from what we may tell—alive, the university has employed me for decades to foster this creativity in their writing. They, not unlike others of the same mistake, seem to think that "creativity" is "fancy," whatever strikes their damaged imaginations as clever, even though it was done better in *Guardians of the Galaxy* (one of the wittier of the comic-book movies). When my students talk about writing, they like to talk about movies—not even "films" but movies, which are without standards and often as poorly written as many critically acclaimed novels.

Creativity, however, demands tradition, a knowledge and experience of what has come before and has been judged significant by time and intellect, combined with the burdens of "talent," which is both a gift from the great gene pool combined with its biblical meaning of a "means of exchange" (e.g., money). Skill helps, too, as well as a highly critical self-awareness: skill is repetition, the practice of doing, done over and over and, yes, over again, gaining the ability to write a word after a word and know it is right, at least until the skilled person applies the rules of talent and discovers that the means—the right word—of exchange does not communicate with his imagined audience. And one must have, as the poet James Merrill once said, his "one perfect reader," at the very least; his one perfect group of readers being preferable; his vast numbers of readers being a thing that he will not aspire to, especially in the age of denigrating commerce where a speech by Martin Luther King might be used to try to sell a pickup truck on television or where, as Greene's "The Invisible Japanese Gentlemen" makes plain, editors and publishers stroke the vanities of writers by praising their "powers of observation" when they don't even notice seven Japanese Gentlemen dining within twenty feet of them.

Tradition demands humility: the student who reads what is assigned and asks not "Do I like this?" but "Why would a professor assign this book for me to read and discuss?"

Here again we have a double problem, the irony that supposes a double audience, one party who doesn't hear and understand but takes the surface as meaning and another party who is aware of the meaning below the surface as well as the first party's incomprehension. Since the sixties we have insisted more and more on the value of our own individual notions and tastes, even if uneducated, unreasoned, or completely without basis or merit. As a result, professors have, in an attempt, perhaps, to be "relevant" (i.e., not bored or boring) applauded writing by less-than-capable writers that serves established agenda. Writing that does not disturb—as good writing ought—or cause the attentive reader to rethink but rather pats him on the back and says, "That's good, Ducky, you are thinking rightly." No, actually not "rightly" but "right," a predicate adjective, not an adverb, because it is not thinking at all but a reinforcement of unnuanced or unprovable notions that have been iconized as "correct."

Professors ought not to profess agendas but to assign books because they are good books, well written and, in the process of selecting, essentially anonymous (and genderless). If you were to assign novels from the twentieth century, you would assign *Mrs. Dalloway* and *To the Lighthouse, Passage to India, The End of the Affair, The Death of the Heart, Waterland, Light in August, A Gathering of Old Men, 100 Years of Solitude,* and you probably would feel obliged to include *The Old Man and the Sea*—among many others, of course. You ought to teach *The Nigger of the Narcissus,* but if you're a so-called White professor, or even an Indian mixblood like me, even if you're Black (refusing the awkward bureaucratic designation of "of color," which means "colored," which was a word Stokely Carmichael wanted us all to drop, substituting "Black," with which I am comfortable even though I know there is all manner of "Black-ness" just as there is all manner of misnomered "Indian-ness"), you dare not because of the almost fascist iconography of "correctness." The test of "purity."

Once, a young woman spotted Randall Kennedy's *Nigger: The*

Strange Career of a Troublesome Word on my office bookshelves and turned against me in horror as though I were William Luther Pierce III. The look on her face would have been priceless, though it hardly altered even after I assured her that Randall Kennedy was indeed Black and a professor at Harvard and that the book was not advocating racism or white supremacy, except for the very fact that her facial expression—and her subsequent pulling back from me as one of her favorite professors—represented the loss of considered thinking that comes with censoring language.

Consider this: A person who calls another human being a nigger accomplishes a number of things rhetorically. He lets you know that he lacks human sympathy and understanding, that his historical sense and awareness is more limited than Putin's Pony, that his life and heart contains irrational hatred and limited feeling, and that anything—*any thing*—he says further about relationships and race is not only suspect but also wrongheaded. Knowing him for this kind of Breitbart person allows us to steer clear of him. But a person who does not say "nigger" but only thinks it ("Wow, look at that nigger walking past my house. He may be casing the place. I'd better keep my eye on him until he's out of the neighborhood"), a policeman who shoots an unarmed Black boy several times because he's carrying a toy wooden gun or because he runs when he's told to stop, is vastly more dangerous, like the fault lines of San Andreas that remain ignorable until the violent and shaking moments of destruction.

A man who calls a Black congresswoman "an empty barrel" may as well say "nigger," because in between giving his childish boss times out, that is what his Bostonian self thinks. What does that mean? Should a professor write a book titled "Empty Barrels: The Strange Career of a Nasty Phrase"? And if it were on my bookshelf, would this young woman—a real representative of what we have done to the minds of students—turn away from me as her professor?

The point, or a point, is that our nation has a vast tradition of racism, which is, in large part, based on a verifiable lack of humility. This humility does not ask but allows one to be aware that one might not be right, that one's thoughts and feelings may be suspect. In other words, if one seeks the truth that "flourishes where the student's lamp has shone" (W. B. Yeats), one must give over to the study of what is assigned and read—and, yes, reread, as that is the only way to get what has been given—and read through.

That, of course, is the other problem: professors, brought up in the postsixties' "your opinion matters," unable to separate "opinion," which is based on thought and analysis from "notion," which is just that, notional, assumed, unexamined, and possibly unbelievable, teach that which agrees with their own ideas or fantasies. Indeed, sitting in on a professor's class as an evaluator for his merit and raise, I actually watched as he twisted a film's "meaning" around so that it meant what he wanted it to mean. And when I ask students if they have ever written an essay to agree with the professor's obvious biases, a nonstatistical, anecdotal 95 percent told me that yes, they had. Moreover, they believed that they had done well and received a high mark on the essay because of it.

Of course they have. Only a student with a bright lamp and lots of courage would write a PhD prospectus that went against the grain of the majority of professors in his or her department. Most students are raised like corn (not reared like human beings) to be self-entitled survivors of the educational system that turns them into fodder for the job market—for money, for commerce, for getting out of their parental hairs financially and beginning the long slog of paying off their first mortgage (student loans) while trying to save for their second mortgage (for a house, perhaps).

Go to a recruitment day on campus and parents will inevitably ask, "What jobs will be available to little Donny when he graduates?" Not, Will little Donny be anything that we might call "educated"? With their parents writing a similar background essay—the one that agrees with the economy's obvious biases and which turns college into not an institution for education but an institution for keeping youth out of the job market until there is space for him/her to do something she/he hates, while marrying someone who hates her (or him)—how are students supposed to even find the switch that turns on the lamp for study?

Then there's "relevance." Why, in heaven's name, are we trying to make educational subjects and experiences "relevant"? Relevant to what? It seems ironic that what purveyors of relevance mean is ideas that they wish they could hold without their buckets leaking as they wander wondering, like the cows in Dylan Thomas's story "A Story."

The irony is not simply in the way we look at the surface of things and depend on them as though they have meaning. The irony is in the things themselves because there are no "things," only processes. No whats, only hows. There are no nouns and verbs, except for convenience of statement and possible communication, only gerunds.

For example, one does not love another human being. One is loving toward a human who is being. That may seem an overly subtle distinction, and yet it seems true: one is loving, not "in love" as though love were a pit of despond, and one does not love an entity but a person engaged in the processes of being lovable and possibly loving back. He or she is not a thing, not static or fixed, but continuously changing both in mind and physics—changing location as well as language, changing the ways in which he or she does things.

Or take an accountant or a coal miner: she is not an accountant at all times but only when she is accounting, the same way a coal miner is a miner when he's mining. The rest of the time he is suffering from incipient black lung after chipping away at the dirtiest dying form of energy available (outside of peat), and there is little accounting for that outside of empathizing, of sorrowing for people who call themselves miners of coal.

A writer is not a writer, even if he goes around acting the writer, unless he or she writes. And whatever pleasure one gets from the hard work of writing is in the doing, not in the publication or the praise or the so-called reputation.

Isn't that what's wrong with the Oscars? All those half-baked egos busy egoing?

And it's also what is wrong with the ironizing of education: grades, measurements for a thing that is not a thing. You don't get an education. You begin being and continue becoming educated. It ought to begin with birth and surely it doesn't stop with graduation or with gainful employment but continues for the rest of your life. All educators do—may or can do—is try to goad, move, and stimulate you to want to be educating yourself as well as your children or friends. And in the process, they, too, engage with educating themselves more or further, which means no lesson plans, no set lectures, but give and take and take and give. Which, believe me, is bloody exhausting, and in creative writing, where there is so much writing and so little that is creative because it is uninformed by the past, the less-than-certain giving and taking, the implicit or explicit criticism, and the demand to work harder and revise endlessly is often unpopular. Students who are entities or things want you to tell them, "This is how you do it. This is how you write a story, poem, essay, or letter home asking for money."

Ironically, unless they engage in the doing, revising, rewriting, throwing away and redoing all over again, unless they engage in the joy that comes from writing a sentence or word that they really like and the realization that they may then have to discard that very sentence or phrase because a part of writing is inviting your one perfect reader to engage with you, the imagined writer writing and the sentence or word that you wrote does not do that . . .

Teaching—educating—is a lot like that: you could try this, you might try that. That's the best a teacher can do, and he always has to listen, not to "I was trying to do this or that" but to "I was trying," to which, if the trying moves away from surface toward depth of understanding and compassion and linguistic charm, is all he may ask for. And when you win, you win together, just as when you lose you do so together, too, and only if the team is fun, then the process is worth it. It is not ironic.

5

PROCESSES FOR BEING

A Whole Lot of Schloss

Walking home from school, Clara is tense and still rattled by Vapide's rudeness to her bumpa by his uninterest in life as in stories and his interneted lack of imagination. The Bronx cheer he gave at the way the story ended makes her quiver with annoyance. Vapide, I say, wants stories to rise and fall and end in a wrap-up sort of way, a way that allows teller and listener alike to forget the body of the story, and what they talk about when they talk about stories is plot, not process.

"Your aunt is coming for a visit," I tell her.

"Goody." It's been a while since her aunt—great-aunt, really—has allowed herself out of the bubble of New York and traveled all two hours by Delta to Detroit.

"You want to go with me to pick her up?"

She doesn't hesitate. No "I've got homework" or "Olivia's coming for a playdate." She sees the hour and a half alone in a car with Bumpa during which she may talk uninterrupted, and Clara, besides running literally everywhere, likes nothing more than to talk.

Bean's great-aunt lives in a junior-ell apartment in Riverdale, just north of New York City. Bean's cousin, who is twenty-six, also lives in New York and rents a tiny bedroom from a young couple engaged to be married, one of whom has suggested a sexual three-way, which makes Bean's cousin (as well as the rest of the family) uncomfortable. While the couple's marriage ceremony approaches, the cousin has been looking for a place to share with a coworker at her new job. She works for a start-up company that services well-heeled young males with "woke" gift packages, which they accept or send back monthly and for which they pay a rather high fee. A present every month because, gosh darn it, they work hard and deserve treats.

It's a sign of the immediate spoiling of the young professional in a city that the spoiled children of fraudulent real estate developers can inherit $435 million and lose much of it in spurious, ill-conceived real estate projects, thus requiring corrupt and racist Daddy to corrupt his racist son with loans that bail him out but that never get repaid. Thus develops a lifetime habit of stiffing renters, contractors, and the IRS by overpricing deductions while undervaluing properties. But hey, his name is on the buildings he doesn't own and couldn't profitably operate, just like his empire of bankrupt golf courses on which he can play and cheat, and when Forbes leaves him off the list of the wealthiest men in our country, he grabs the tiny tip of his finger and plays with himself while calling Forbes to insist he be added.

Finding an affordable apartment to rent in New York is impossible now, and a recent *New York Times* op-ed suggests that young professionals are finding out that they not only are happy moving to rural America but that a majority of them also say that they are happier, the inevitable comparative for young people who do not want to become as selfish as Putin's Puppet and who are content to speak for themselves in the rural barbershops and coffeehouses, or the brick-and-mortar or farmers' markets of their neighbors and friends—or at least agreeable acquaintances who no longer believe that tariffs on Chinese goods are paid by the Chinese and not them. They know that the retaliatory tariffs on American farm goods and equipment have reduced their incomes to such an extent that family farms and jobs are being lost at a rate unmatched by anything outside of Guatemalan children at our southern border.

Nearly thirty years ago, Bean's nana and bumpa moved from New York City to Michigan, to the very lower tier center of the state. On your right hand, held up flat, as Michiganders like to do, East Lansing would take its position around two-thirds of your life line.

Nana was distressed. Her family lived in New York City, and family, to the descendent of Italians, was everything. Indeed, the whole reason she agreed to move was so she could afford to have a family of her own. New York City already was expensive, requiring the sale of your firstborn child to afford your rent.

Bumpa was pleased by the move, though not a little bored. After all, he was Indian—the kind that allows him to suggest that White immigrants chanting "Send her back" ought themselves to consider going back to the lands from which they came armed with rifles, disease, and bad faith to an open land where they made deals they didn't have to pay for or keep.

He wasn't a Michigan Indian. His grandfather had been gathered up like an illegal immigrant and imprisoned in a boarding school in a region that was flatter and hotter than the mountain valleys, where one day the children were assembled and told to pick a surname from the names posted on a white board and he picked ours.

Or so one story went.

The other rendition was that at a boarding school run by Quakers—people who shake in spiritual reveries and who feel called upon (by whom?) and moved to rise and speak—a Quaker missionary married a Nez Perce woman, thereafter creating the quiet, stoic grandson who one hot afternoon in Napa, California, answered his grandson's "What do I do, Grandfather?" with "I don't know. But watch your immigration laws."

It was a joke. Our joke. A cartoon that Grandfather kept that showed Indians who, asked by European invaders what advice they had to give, reply, "Be careful with your immigration laws." A joke that the people who think there are good people on both sides of Charlottesville demonstrations forget the Trail of Tears or the Osage murders or the slaughters by their esteemed general Custer emptying the Great Plains of anyone and anything, like buffalo or unfenced land, along with the caravans of migrant Natives.

What do I do, Grandfather?

In the aftermath of laughter, I've forgotten what I may have been referring to. Grandfather, though knowing, did not see fit to let more than a tadpole of bitterness seep out. He edited his stories, so it was a tadpole that was not meant to turn his grandson bitter but to remind him—always—to be skeptical of his own and others' motives, not to distrust treaties per se but to wonder at why among honorable and honest people they needed to be made, and to hold tight to the vision of the need for band, for family, for going forward as far as one might go, of remaining engaged in the process not of return but of re-creation.

There is no return. And re-creation does not aim at reiteration.

There is the land, the air, the waters, but there is no identifiable geographical place for an Indian removed from his seasons where you may point to on a map and say, "Here, here is where I belong and where I want to establish borders that I will protect to keep this static place mine."

There is no "mine," though the word may be used as though it means something: "my" wife, "my" daughter or son, "my" son-in-law, "my" granddaughter or grandson. But the pronoun of possession is precisely that: a pro-noun. "Pro-," the word-forming element that means "before" or "forward" and "noun." Nouns are used to identify, but that identification is virtually meaningless—I was going to say "outside of physics," but I realize that nouns are almost entirely meaningless in physics. An atom is not a thing but a movement and a field.

Okay, what about your edgy friend, Brunhilde? Same answer: she is not a thing but a process, reducible to a series of processes, perhaps, but nonetheless.

Or what is "my life"?

"I" have no "life." I am a gerund, I am living, and I have had living-ness occur, but none of the living-ness may be adequately separated and discretely described without the need and nuance of verb. I am, in other words, "me, doing" and even when I tell Clara Bean stories that I hope mean and hope carry with them, the love I feel for her and her brother, Char-char (Charlie), the doing is the important part.

As Shakespeare wrote (and often gets misinterpreted the way I am purposely doing), "What's in a name?"

The answer is that it isn't the discrete name that matters but the genetic inheritance contained in the history of that name: you might be Capulet or Montague, but you are being Capulet or Montague, and what is in a name is that love or marriage between them isn't going to be allowed to work. "A rose by any other name would smell as sweet," which only goes to show how conveniently meaningless the word "rose," in this context, is. A Capulet by any other name would smell as Capulet, perhaps, but his Capuletic épée would be as sharp and deadly.

My life, then, is not a thing. It is a set of attitudes and relationships and endless small doings that may not be placed in a bucket or fish tank or museum display case but only passed along and, in the passing, reach back to all the passings that have passed before and join these passings to what passeth and to come, and a Nez Perce has—because of this processional connection and history—a pretty good idea of what will be allowed to come.

These attitudes or relationships may be given but given only as stories, regardless of how sweet or bitter they may smell. The stories may be given titles, as essays may, but story they are, narrative processes locked in individual contexts both large and small.

So when Bean's round face turns up, and she says, "Tell me a story about New York, Bumpa," I have to think about what I want to be allowed to come and what may be or should be relegated to the story-telling bin of "forgettery," if I want what will come to be for her and not for me, memoried expectation of future, not fixed memory of what I think should be let go.

When we lived in New York, Nana found us a one-bedroom apartment on 176th Street. Our upstairs neighbors were named Schloss. At a right angle to our front door was the door to one Mrs. Bergman.

The Schlosses were apartment-size people. Short. Small. Could fit in anywhere and still leave room for a sofa and loveseat. Mrs. Schloss spoke with a heavy accent left over from 1930s Germany and transposed onto a late-learned English. Mr. Schloss, slightly rotund, spoke very little to anyone besides her. Whether he knew English or not, I never knew, given that he always let his wife and partner do the talking for both of them.

Abraham Schloss wobbled when he walked, as though each foot fell to a lower step. They went everywhere together, letting themselves out of the heavy glass doors from our foyer with its elevator in the mornings, wheeling behind them a wire shopping basket that often seemed empty when Abraham Schloss stepped back up onto the low marble step to the foyer doors and, with a mighty apartment-size heave, lifted the few things they'd acquired in their perambulations up and through the doors she held open for him.

They were happy. Pleased to be together, matched in size and heart and, for all I knew, in mind, both joyful to wake up in the mornings without Ida Schloss's being ordered off with the other women to the laundry or Abe Schloss's marching off with men to break up granite rocks with a sledgehammer. They rose, ate, and left the building to once again search out the few things they needed to fill their stomachs or protect them from the rain. More than happy or pleased, they were committed. They knew what it meant to be kept apart. They survived. Now they were together and, like doves, would always be.

I often watched the pair of them trundle down 176th Street as I cooled off in front of the window's air conditioner after forty-five minutes on my rowing machine. Not infrequently, I saw them return, Mr. Schloss reaching the exact same spot on the sidewalk and waiting for her to unlock and open the door, placing his feet with the exact same wobble and fix that he had used yesterday, as though there were footprints painted on the sidewalk for him to place his feet upon. Standing at bent and rapt attention.

Sometimes I'd be leaning out the window, trying to squeegee the globs of wet bagel Mr. Schloss dropped down to the perching pigeons. During New York summers, if I didn't clean off the globs every day, they baked onto the unit and I'd have to pull it in from the window and scrape it with a putty knife. I blamed the pigeons for Abraham's wet bagels and I hated them and their incessant cooing with the calm intensity of an allergic person who hates cats.

The Schlosses were dear, sweet, and far from wealthy. From what Mrs. Schloss said, I gathered that even the wet bagel pieces Abe dropped out his window to feed the pigeons were day old and discounted. They were a sacrifice, a small one, like a person short of money giving to Feeding America.

Unlike our next-door neighbor who one morning asked me to rid her apartment of bats, I'd never entered their apartment. Mrs. Bergman's apartment was a stereotype of tchotchkes and silver-framed photographs, the chintz and blintz of so many widowed apartments in New York. As it turned out, her bat was a large flake of peeling paint that had folded down from the ceiling. Frightened the bat would take flight and lodge in her thinning poof of hair, she had built up her courage, come over, knocked, and asked. I left a puddle of water on my air conditioner to soak into the bagel pieces and, reassuring her that it was no trouble at all, followed her across the hall. For a brief moment, I stood in the doorway gazing at her ceiling, wondering at the flake of paint that hung down and flapped in the circulating air of her apartment's stifling heat.

Trying to convince her of the truth would take too long, so I asked to borrow a broom. She lent me an angled broom and at my direction sequestered herself in the bedroom with the door closed. I opened the living room window and, with noises that would sound like a man chasing and swatting at a darting, swooping bat, carefully swept the paint peel off the ceiling and put it into the hallway to take to the garbage. Then I showed Mrs. Bergman her clean ceiling. The bat, I told her, had flown out the window past the pecking pigeons toward the heavy shade of maples lining avenues to the south.

Was I supposed to tell her it wasn't a bat? Why? It would be, I thought, like telling stories to a child that she needn't hear, stories that did not create opportunity but possibly invited imitation. Moreover, why would anyone want to force a woman diminished by her years and loneliness to admit to yet another loss, of eyesight and awareness?

Mrs. Bergman was, in fact, nearly blind, her eyes reduced like her olfactory senses that let her ignore the food burning on her stove in her kitchen while failing to notice flames rising from the frying oil on her gas stovetop. She worried the super. She worried me. Just the month before, a nearby building burned down because a tenant had set an electric defroster ring going in her freezer and then left the house. She returned to find her possessions, along with her yappy dog, turned to ash, her neighbors milling together on the sidewalk, and firemen with their heavy hoses cleaning up.

For the next week, of course, I received paper plates filled with unrecognizable home-baked goods, rugelach and hamantashen, burned butter-free cookies, nut-free almond crackers, and leftover sesame bagels from Zabar's. Late at night, I slipped down to the basement dumpster. Still, I would no more have told Mrs. Bergman that she was blind and deaf than I would tell Clara Bean about the laundry or the chain gang the Schlosses survived before immigrating to the United States, nor what the numbers tattooed on their wrists meant. Not at her age. Not during childhood, "when the world is puddle-wonderful" "in Just-spring." Later, maybe, when she's old enough to hear what people can do to people, how her fellow Americans forget history or make ignorance normal by calling the truth "fake."

So what do I say when Bean asks for stories?

I tell her about the day the bag man took up camping in the foyer of our building, glossing over the fact that no one should have to live like that in a country as lucky as ours. Making a joke about the fact that Mr. and Mrs. Schloss were "apartment size," able to fit easily into a one-bedroom flat upstairs in Washington Heights, north of Harlem. "Indeed," I say, "their diminutive height and size made them a perfect fit." Squeezing her small hand, I add, "Like you." I hold her hand lightly but firmly, ready to grab her when her motor revs too high and her clutch slips, popping her into running gear.

Bean runs. Everywhere and all the time, unless you hold her back, and even then she moves in fits and starts, darting ahead, stopping, and darting back to you. Many are the days I hear her back door slam (they live next door) and see Clara Bean shoot off the patio deck to the half acre of lawn behind her house and run around the perimeter, her knees bending and her feet kicking up behind her in joy. After a circuit or two, she may stop to swing on the play structure we put in, catching her breath before hopping down and running back inside. Even on the mornings I walk her to school, she dashes across the lawn, stopped only by the potential for stories and the fact that at seventy, the image of Bumpa running resembles the Tin Man in the Wizard of Oz. Recently, I found myself in a dream at night fully aware in the dream that I was dreaming and all because I was—in the dream—running with the bounce and stride that attracted my high school's cross-country coach. When I awoke, I was relieved to find myself lying in bed.

"Am I apartment size?"

I nod.

"Will I always be?"

"Doubt it."

"Why not?"

"Well, for one you're already the height of a solitary Schloss."

"I'm five," says she. "And a half."

"More than a half. Five and ten months," I say, and Bean sort of leans back on her heels and smiles.

"Anyway, one day I was looking out my front window watching the people waiting for the bus that might not come, and I saw Mr. and Mrs. Schloss make their wobbly way up 176th."

Clara laughs. She likes the alliteration of "wobbly way," and whether these tricks of language work or not, I am always in search of things to make her laugh. She flips, walking backward, looking up at me and waiting. She already knows, well, how Abraham Schloss took pleasure in feeding the pigeons, tossing pieces of wet day-old bagel out his window, pieces that most often plopped onto my protruding air conditioner, attracting flights of pigeons to perch and peck and wake me up in the bright morning with their collective coo. On the day after the local bakery sold off its leftover stock of bagels, the pigeons pecking outside were so thick and fluttery that people waiting for the bus had to wave and shoo to reach the curb. Even the Cholula sauce I spread on my air conditioner did little other than give the pigeons diarrhea and force pedestrians into a special vigilance. I did try gently to question Mrs. Schloss about the bagels, asking her if she, too, had a problem with someone dropping pieces of wet bagel on her air conditioner. She raised her eyebrows and said something to Abraham in Yiddish; he shrugged, splaying out his hands as though catching a ball as if to say, *Who knows?* "Sorry," she said, ignoring my meaningful stare at her carry-all filled with day-old bread. "By the way," she added, "I've been meaning to ask. Do you golf?"

The first time I told Clara this, she was as easily distracted as Mrs. Schloss might have wished, saying, "You do, don't you, Bumpa?"

"I do. But I didn't then."

"Why not?"

"I wasn't old then."

Distractions, however, are a part of the process of telling. Distractions, as long as you aren't sitting at a stoplight impeding progress, often lead to other stories and their morals—in this case how I determined that what Mrs. Schloss referred to as "golf" had to be my rowing machine on the parquet sounding like someone rolling a golf ball around and around. It made me more considerate, rowing at times the Schlosses should be deep in sleep in another room or in middle mornings when my neighbors were well awake and might be less disturbed by the repetitive sounds of exercise. The moral pleasure of neighborly consideration.

"As I watched them," I tell Clara, "the Schlosses approached the heavy glass doors to our building and then stopped, turned, and moved back out to the edge of the curb. Mrs. Schloss said something to Abraham, who shrugged, raising his hands as if to ask, *What am I to do?* They milled there, from time to time gazing through the door glass before returning to the curb. A pigeon flapped down and strutted on my air conditioner, tilting its eye at me as though to inquire where breakfast was and why was it late. Something clearly was up, and I went downstairs.

"There I found a homeless man hunkered in the corner, his wheeled wire shopping cart and blankets piled in front of him. He was muttering and gesturing with angry facial expressions and waving hands. As much as I object to anyone being homeless in a country as rich as ours, I gave him my best New York look, the look that says, *Don't tread on me*, to quiet him. Then I went out, gathered the Schlosses and their hold-all filled with bread for my air conditioner and, taking Mrs. Schloss's arm, led them inside, past the homeless man, and into the elevator. I rode up with them to their floor. Abraham offered me a bagel as thanks, which I declined, saying, 'I'm sure I'll get some soon,' causing him to look confused as he stepped out of the elevator and the doors slid shut."

"Did you?" Clara asks.

"Did I what?"

"Get some bagels? Like Mrs. Bergman's hamantossers."

I don't correct her. "I got a lot more than that. For months, I'd been cursing the neighbor who dropped wet bread onto my air conditioner. I'd even thought about going upstairs to confront him next time it happened."

"What did you get?"

"Tolerance," I reply, thinking that this isn't the way a Native story should end. But then this wasn't a Native story, merely a story told by a Native. "It was like a beacon. I got more light from it than it got from me.

"Once the Schlosses were safe in their apartment above the man who golfed, I turned round and went back down to the foyer to see the homeless man. 'Listen,' I told him, 'I don't know if you'll understand, but you need to go somewhere else.'

"He lifted his head like an old dog and growled.

"'Growl if you must. But if I call the super, he'll call the cops. I don't want the cops called any more than you do.' I had seen the cops with the homeless, poking them with their batons and prodding them out and up the street like lonely cattle, giving these miserable dropouts from getting and spending no quarter, no chance, no space in which to be.

"It was as though I'd held the back of my hand out and down, allowing him to sniff me and determine how big a threat I was. He stopped growling and, nodding, muttering to himself, rose and gathered his blanket and sleeping bag into his wire cart. I held the door open for him. I watched him slide up the sidewalk for a second and then, on impulse, caught up to him and handed him the little cash I carried. I did not tell him to buy some food or to find a rescue mission to sleep in. Just gave him the cash. I knew where he'd spend it and on what. But I hoped that, as the fortified wine warmed his insides, for a moment he'd feel as though his plastic bags were from Nordstrom and his Mogen David was equal to a five-martini lunch."

And that was not just how it was but was how it ought to be.

CARBON TO CHARCOAL

The problem with paths is not that one is more traveled than the other—they are, really, about the same. It's that once you've chosen to go up or down a particular path, you are stuck with it. You are condemned to travel through all nine circles of the Inferno, even if your guide or traveling companion is not Virgil but a five-year-old dancing bubble of love and joy on a fine sunshiny day whose name is Bean. It did not take a great deal of wisdom for me to foretell that once she'd drawn "Balls and Bumpas" out of me, she'd pirouette to carbon.

Wisps of her fine brown hair catch the light where it's come loose from the bobby-pinned curls around the singular thin braid from ear over to ear, and her eyes squint with excitement as she hands off her turquoise backpack to me. Grabbing my hand she tows me away from the school's fortifications and the mothers hovering, waiting for one child to tie and retie her shoes, or another to fold his failures at abstract art, or a third, still having difficulties with telling "left" from "right," to retrace his steps and reach the exit door. And this is a warm fall day. I can hardly wait for winter, if winter indeed comes, when it will take fifteen minutes longer for children to complete their sartorial tasks going to and coming from school. Even little mainstreamed Ciaran with his dedicated teacher's aide will take for freaking ever. But not Bean. Bean has been planning her escape for hours. She is trained by her parents to order her actions and, more importantly, to stick to the order, completing tying her boots before becoming distracted by a wasp banging out its life against a high Safeguard window. She washes her hands habitually, which I, being older and more susceptible to the virulent germs of youth, appreciate. Even then, the petri dish called elementary school is able to slip by our safeguards from time to time.

"Bumpa," Bean shouts, dashing across the edges of the lawn to throw her arms around my right leg, crashing into my knee as I lean down and squeeze her back against it.

"How was school?" I ask.

"Fine," she says, already turning her eyes toward a gaggle of bigger kids jogging down the long street that runs past the high school, then the elementary a mile down. Once they pass the middle school across the street from the elementary, they're supposed to pass bobsled hill, the high school's baseball diamond, and circle the broad expanses of grass on which the high school's football team practices its training for CTE.

"What did you do today?"

"More project," she replies. She skips off after a maple leaf slip-sliding down from the trees that are turning. She knows I know that the "project" is her teacher's periodic attempts to make the children aware of their family histories. She also knows I want her to feel connected to the Indian attitudes of my grandfather. But she's smart enough to realize that when the family tells stories, my stories tend to skip the generation that was my parents'. I rarely talk about my father, and only with Clara's prodding do I realize that I never speak of my mother. Like an unbalanced barbell, Clara's family history project is heavy with Dutch and Italians on one end, with the lone figure of a Nez Perce grandfather holding its own on the other. But after school, Bean wants to ask. I can feel her wanting to ask, yearning like a sunflower for the warming light of sunshine.

"Good ahead," I say as I throw the straps of her backpack over my shoulder. "Ask."

She stretches. She feels the release. Thinks. "What was your mommy like?"

Not like yours. That's for sure. "What do you mean?"

"I mean what was she like?" Bean says, squinting at me.

"She was a mommy." Of sorts.

"Bum-paaa."

I shrug. An apology of sorts.

"What kinds of things did your mommy say?"

"Carbon's good for you," I blurt. It just comes out.

Clara Bean stopped skipping, waited for me to catch up, and looked up at me. She has this wide-open questioning look that she's learned to give me, right before she asks me if I'm teasing. Bumpa teases a lot. Not teases her, but teases as in joking, making as light of the heavy world she's got coming as he can. It's what bumpas do.

"Is it?"

"What?"

"Good for you."

I had to think about that. It's the problem with teasing, joking. You may bring up something you've not thought about for a long time and your granddaughter may ask you to explain with the same seriousness her mother conveyed when she asked me how I knew the black squirrel was named Frankie while the brown was named Stuart and that, yes, that black squirrel is, obviously, Frankie and not just some indiscriminate squirrel on our way to the park.

"Carbon is important. Twenty percent of you is carbon."

"So your mommy was right?"

"I guess she was, in a way."

Bean clamped her mouth shut and went all quiet. Her way of telling me that she expects more than this. She wants a story, even a brief walking-home story—which are, often, the best stories, grains of sand inside an oyster that can layer it as it gets retold over and over, making it luminescent and precious. Story, in addition to teasing, is another thing bumpas do, with the hope that the story will guide or teach, analyze or reveal with the lightness of an offer instead of instruction, especially bumpas descended from the wonderful Nez Perce storyteller, Mary Blue.

A problem with stories is that they have to begin and end. Mary Blue emphasized process, which is why many of her stories ended "And that was the way it was" or "That's how it was," turning the story's end back on the story's telling and being listened to, the connection and bond that is formed between teller and listener, and the listener and all the tellers who have come before. A story like that allows for the singular semi-discrete story to join together with all the stories that offer the process of how one ought to be not just now but forever. A Coyote story teaches while it joins the audience to all Coyote stories, from which the listener may learn how to behave around Coyote, who is a creative but very tricky force.

But a storyteller does not want to injure Coyote and take away all the mischievous fun and endless creativity. Thus he has cautiously to cut a segment of the ongoing thread that is life, one that is a manageable size, not too short for the auditor's involvement and not so long that it will tangle or stick like the filaments of a spider's web in the teller's inventing mind.

Any story I might tell Bean about my mother engages me in so much pain and confusion that it seems doomed to be too long, replete with backtracking and modifications as she asks her five-year-old's questions and demands her five-year-old's augmentations and explanations.

The shortest version, that my mother was so bad a cook that she burned nearly everything so that it became a joke of connection among her children, might amuse me, but it is insufficient for her need for family history.

The longer version that Mother was bitter, unfulfilled, unhappy in her marriage, for possibly good reason, and took her anger at all of it out on the food she shoved in front of Father and us threatens to become unwieldy, tangled and confused, needing story after story to correct, modify, alter, or add to what has been told, a process like labeling the bones of a Halloween skeleton, with as little reality. I've noticed that like all old people the problem of separating and isolating details, of sorting the meaningful from the unimportant and then sticking to the meaningful as I tell a story, has become increasingly difficult as everything seems to connect, everything that connects seems to be important, and everything important can lead me off along a path less traveled, even though really about the same. I am becoming no better than the old lady who, telling you why the parents of choirboys are picketing the church of a pedophile priest, slips into describing where she parked her Toyota and ends with wondering aloud whether or not it is time to replace her five-year-old Corolla, entirely forgetting where and with what intent she began. It's like shopping: one goes to Whole Foods for wild-caught salmon and sees fresh asparagus on sale as he enters, and the week's menus change and fall apart.

"Bumpa?"

"What? Oh, sorry. With me and my sisters, 'carbon's good for you' became a joke because my mother was proficient at burning food. She could even burn toast in the automatic toaster, turning up the darkness dial and waiting until black smoke rose up from the slots for bread. She burned everything, at least before her . . . before Father left."

"Where did he go?"

"That's another story," I say quickly, cutting her off. I don't want to try to explain divorce. It happens, for good or for ill, but it won't happen in Bean's family.

"Anyway. Night after night we'd sit down at the dinner table and Mother would set plates of what she insisted was edible food product in front of us. We'd stare at the plates, dilatorily pushing around what we imagined to be burned fragments of broccoli or beans looking for edible morsels. In my family, knives were not so much used for cutting up as they were to cut out, to sever green and white from the crispy deep, dark black of food cremated by Mother's frustration and her anger at being expected to cook for her family.

"'Eat your food,' she'd say, pointing her fork at the piles of burned matter that built up on the edge of our plates.

"'But it's burned.'

"'Maybe it's a little overdone. But there are children in Africa who'd give their lives to have food like this.'

"Night after night, year after year, these African children hovered around our family's dinner table until I finally got so sick of them that I brought a shipping carton to the table. I offered to pack my dinner up and pay to have it sent to those African children.

"'It'd cost a fortune,' Mother insisted. 'Besides,' she said, 'carbon's good for you.'

"I did look up carbon in the green bound *Funk and Wagnall's Encyclopedia*, which Mother purchased by subscription. I learned that we—you, me, everyone—are made up partly of carbon. That carbon is a chemical that combines with other chemicals to form some of the necessary ingredients of life.

"I took it to heart. At the time, I had two dogs. Rusty, a beagle mix with a few brains, and Butchy, a blond mutt with fewer brains than a swamp rat at Mar-a-Lago. I spent hours with them and my Tonka truck in the barren dirt behind our garage. They kept me company, their snouts turned up and their tails sweeping the dirt with expectation and hope. I fed them Fives dog biscuits. Fives came in five flavors, meat, vegetable, cheese, charcoal, and ginger. I tried them all. The meat and vegetable ones tasted too much like mother's Thanksgiving. The cheese and ginger seemed pretty much the same. The black charcoal ones were the best.

"I gave all the red and yellow, dark green, and pale green biscuits to Rusty and Butchy. I ate all the black. They were supposed to contain carbon enough to keep my teeth clean without brushing, but I ate them because I liked them. Eating them was comforting, as though a nice family meal."

"We have family meals," Clara says, her lips spread into a smile revealing a grille of teeth.

"Yes, you do. Nice ones. The food your mommy gives you is good and healthy and it tastes good, like your nana's."

"So what else?"

"What else what else?"

"Your mommy. Did she mind your eating Rusty and Butchy's biscuits?"

"Not really. When she found out, she called the doctor and asked him what he thought and he said it couldn't really hurt me. There wasn't very much carbon in the charcoal Fives.

"I guess too much carbon and you can end up dehydrating yourself or interfering with the inevitable process of your becoming a fossil fuel."

Clara frowns and then decides that this must be some kind of a joke. She likes jokes. For a year or more her favorite has been, "Tell me,

Bumpa, does a changer make cents?" She calls the checkout clerks at Whole Foods "changers."

We turn off Burcham onto Knoll Road, ascending the up of the up-and-over street to its intersection with our street at the bottom. Like a puppy smelling home, she pulls against the leash of my hand until I let go of hers and tell her to go ahead. "Just watch for cars." It's a winding street that goes nowhere after beginning nowhere, so there's not much danger of seeing a car. Without her backpack, Bean will run most of the way down to her grandma's house on the right, three houses shy of Bumpa's and four shy of her own on the other side, before turning around and running back to me. If I don't stop her, she'll then repeat the process. For one thing Bean does and likes to do is run. I've looked out my bedroom window to see her run across our lawn, legs churning in her pink tights to give a crash hug to Nana, her eyes turned up to spot the falcons hunting robins and sparrows. Our puppy loves her to go along for walks, getting double the exercise running down to the stop sign and back, stopping only for the few cars that enter our neighborhood.

Hardly winded, she returns to my side. "What else was your mommy like?" Before I can answer, she's off again.

Afraid. Of men, for one, and their anger or disapproval. Night after night when I was at college, I listened to her go on about the men who taught with her at school, how they expected her to do everything and criticized her for the ways she did them. She hated men because of her fear, and when I flew home to visit her and discovered that she had given away the two cartons of antique HO trains I stored in her garage, I had to fight to laugh. She got rid of all my things, even though I was only gone to college, and when I questioned her, she accused me of leaving, justifying her bitter actions with "Well, you weren't here."

Another time, I made a special trip home to surprise her on a day she was having my sister and her husband to lunch. She made a point of telling me there was food in the fridge, if I needed, and then closed the door, leaving me in her television room with the two dogs. The next time I came home was for her memorial service before which my eldest sister scattered her ashes in the dog run at the back of the yard and after which I made a joke like "carbon's good for you." A woman insisted, "Your mother was such a lovely person," and it took all my self-control not to reply, "You didn't know her well, I guess."

When Father told me at ten that my birth had ruined his marriage, did she defend me? When I drove her five hundred miles to visit her father and his third wife, and he sat me in a corner and never spoke to me or used my name but made it plain he loathed my existence, did she explain why on the long drive home from John Birch country?

Did she ever consider that telling me I could get run over by inattentive drivers as I crossed Strathern Street to home might paralyze me with fear when one afternoon, in the deluge of rain from the monsoon lashing North Hollywood, I slipped in the five-inch churn of water and fell into the gutter? I lay there expecting at any moment to be crushed by the wide tires of a 1950s Plymouth. My legs were frozen and my cries unheard beneath the noisy plash of water. All I could move was my arms. I managed to stretch them to the curb and, digging my fingers into the grass of the parking strip, pulled my pudgy, soaking body inch by inch up onto the puddles of grass where, safe, I lay panting until after several minutes my legs worked and I got up. Letting the sheets of rain wash me clean I crossed through our backyard and entered the house where Mother demanded to know what I'd done to my new pink-and-black striped T-shirt. When I told her, panting from the re-creation of the scene, she said, "You should be more careful." The same thing she said when I was eight and she slammed my fingers in the hinge of the Plymouth's heavy door as I hurried to get in.

I learned to refuse to let fear incapacitate. If old and former fears began to creep up my spine, I stopped, held myself still, breathed deeply and slowly, using all my sense and reason to push it down. By the time I was eleven, when my eldest sister miscarried while her husband searched for towels in a panic, I calmly phoned an ambulance.

When my other sister's ape of a boyfriend pressed his drunken face to my midnight window, having climbed the fence and mistaken my window for my sister's, I slid open the window and told him to go away. And watched him lurch like Quasimodo out into the darkness.

But much later, when my friend Steve, detrained and out scrounging wood for a warming fire, looked up as the couplings of our boxcar clanged tight and the train began lurching forward, and Steve began to run toward the boxcar in which I stood, fear never crossed my mind. I removed my parka to bare my arm, braced myself against the metal strap across the open door, decided not to reach for Steve's wavering hand but to grasp his forearm as he grasped mine. Coupled with reimagined athleticism and trust, Steve leapt up at the moving boxcar as I reached down and without thinking pulled him up under the metal strap and into the car in one smooth motion. Had I missed, had I felt frightened or confused, had either of us been less certain, Steve would never have become the surfer poet "dancing the waves" of Hawaii.

Only at moments has that ingrained fear reared its Gorgon head, moments like when Bean's mommy toddled down the slope toward the edge of the Cliffs of Moher in County Clare, Ireland, and I firmly grabbed her belt and kept her distant—very distant—from what felt like the edge of the world. Anyone who has ever looked out from those cliffs, seagulls sweeping the waves below with their cries, knows the world ends there and there is no way a father born from my mother is going to let Miss Oopsie trundle trippingly down toward the split-rail fence without gripping her belt. Though laughed at in what has become a family story, I don't mind because I remain certain privately that I was right to hold her back.

The night Mother died, I sat in my living room as the Syracuse, New York, sky unburdened itself of foliage, trying to convince myself that I might have been a difficult son for my mother who hated men. Almost all men: not just her own father, one of the nastiest rich white Republicans who made his fortune buying up what people were forced to sell during the Great Depression; not just her husband, an Indian man frustrated by the lack of sex and affection and his failure to be appreciated or respected or accepted at home or work, who spent free family time crammed into a compact car with four other people, pounding the dashboard and driving madly about to "vacation" in cheap and cheesy cabins that would set a scary Halloween movie. When I emerged like Dante's pilgrim, it was dawn, and in the dim light I saw how I had learned from her to be inattentive to other people, to quash sympathy and empathy, and to be always selfish, even to the point of taking risks most teenagers do not have the opportunity to take. With little or no sense of humor, by the time I got to know her, Mother was afraid of most things. Fear ran her life and she used fear to try to run her children's. Humor was what would henceforth matter. A realization that made Nana possible and in turn Bean's mommy and her uncs, let alone Bean herself. It's why I with most things tease and always look for the better if not the best.

It is why I make up stories, and in the stories I may let Bean love her unknown grandmother. Burning the bones of memory, the carbon, down to the fuel of charcoal that allows the future light and in that way makes carbon good for her.

"So Bumpa?" Bean says, bouncing on her toes. "What?"

"She may have been a lovely woman," I reply. It's the best I can do.

FROM PAPER TO PERSON

I can hear Nana say, loudly, pointedly, "Maybe ask Bumpa if he can help you."

It must be important. Or maybe it's just Nana's way of keeping me involved, the same way she did when it was with our children and not our grandchild. Otherwise, Nana would drop everything and do it herself. She's just that kind of person when it comes to Bean, our oldest grandchild. A dropper and a doer.

I'm a wait-for-later kind of guy. I live in the fantasy of my time being important, or maybe not so much important but occupied. Like Wall Street. Everyone knows how far occupying Wall Street got us. Almost as far as occupying the administration building at Cal: a few newspaper photos of naïve lambs rushing about on little self-important feet, photos that let people who envied Yutes to hate those dirty radicals who went on to become rich with the tides of change.

"Bumpa," Bean calls down the stair to my basement study. "Are you coming up?"

"I'll be up in a bit, sweetheart," I call back. "I just need to finish this."

Whatever "this" is, I think, grinning like the Cheshire Cat. It's a knowing combination of pleasure at the sentence I am writing combined with the grin that spreads out from my heart like olive oil across focaccia at the happy lilt of Beaner's question. She is always asking questions, poking her focus into the ebbs and flows of daily life like an otter.

My grin is a sly, private sort of grin that goes with writing well and thinking, however temporarily, that my sentences or words are just too clever, so clever that they run the rhetorical risk tested only by my personal theory of necessitarianism: Is it necessary? Clever and smart readers who read beyond banality will respond badly, thinking, "He thinks he's just so cute," and not-so-smart readers will look out from their hovels of agenda and say something dumb, like "Heigh ho, heigh ho, something's got to go." Unless it is necessary, it runs a risk I no longer have time to recover from. Like the stock market. You can take a flyer, but don't do it with funds you need to live on for the next four hundred years, which, according to Big Pharma advertisements, is my life expectancy as long as I'm not allergic to living. Similarly, you can take a flyer—be too cute—with sentences and words, but you run the risk of losing your reader, which is worse than losing money.

As with readers, I try to hide this self-regard, turning it into the grateful grin of getting to see Clara Bean most every day. Now that she's well past the challenge and whine of her twos and threes, tall enough no longer to fear my height when I lift her up, a clean and jerk motion, like weights at the gym, she is more fun for Bumpa. Since she was two, she had language, often able to mimic children several years her senior, pronouncing and using correctly words like "silhouette" and "disintegrate," which made the adults in the room very cautious; now, school age, she has not only language but enunciation, too. In other words, she speaks, I listen, and I am able to understand what I am listening to.

In a postverbal world, where people walk around emojifying, not only unable to spell but also unable to think because they do not know the derivation and history of the sign "u" or the meaning of "luv" (How hard would it be to type "love"—one more letter? After all, someone walking around with his head bent to his cellular phone has plenty of time to waste on love) and knowing the Latin or Greek or Romance roots of words may—does—help us understand what it is that we are wanting to say or think or think about. But as 23 percent of Americans do not know that 1776 marks our independence from (a) Britain, (b) Somalia, (c) Poland, (d) other, or (e) all/none of the above, and as 40 percent do not know that 1776 was really in 1776 (after all, that may be "fake news"), the only place for hope is in the individual, in the grandchild of word-full parents and grandparents, combined with the wistful sadness of predicted expectation that said grandchild will be separate from other children her age because of words, facts, history, and thinking or imagining (not fantasizing).

Personal history tells me that Bean will be liked by most of her teachers who are able to understand her speech and who will suffer the joys of teaching to her level rather than to the lowest- and most-common denominator. Possibly—because she is well reared—she will be liked by children who instinctively recognize the advantages of having a friend who can direct traffic outside the school in the right direction and even, if she is generous and willing, able to tutor them in subjects worthy of learning.

Yet inevitably, she will be a loner among the crowd of others, and if she wants to have any friends at all, she will have to dumb down her language as well as her behavior toward the dopamine dullness of modern "life" (my quotation marks are to suggest that I don't think it much of "life" at all but mostly repetition to the point of meaning-less possession and the wasting of natural resources). She will have to edit herself in speech, behavior, and philosophical thinking in order to avoid putting off the dying breed of the middlingly attentive. She will use phrases, when asked, of "Tommy's not so smart" to avoid saying outright that Tommy is as dumb as sawdust even though she will know that "dumb" does not mean, originally, "stupid" but mute, unable to speak off the cuff or plate, "ex tempore" as they say, meaning people who haven't reduced themselves to Twitter or Instagram or Fox News for their philosophical intake.

By "dumb," though, Beaner will not mean "mute" cohorts but those unable to empathize with the way some of us are embarrassed by the way that, evidently, people can manage never to grow up and yet still become president. Those sad people who do not enjoy reading whole books of literature instead of self-help or dealmaking or how to sur-round oneself with the opulent ugliness of a tacky Versailles. (Probably, I ought to edit that out, but old age makes me stubborn. Besides, by writing words, you can't offend people who do not read.)

Should she decide that she is happier being alone than in the middle of the madding crowd, she may turn to paper people like her mother who constructed her own friends, three-foot-tall paper dwarves, colored, cut out, and mounted on stiff cardboard props. Truly.

I am not alone in this.

Watching my own daughter suffer a few slings and arrows of outrageous grammar school was painful in a Watching Papa sort of way. A papa with rules—or really guidelines, since the purpose of a rule is to be broken, but not by much, not by enough to cause hurt or injury, short or long run. The overarching goal was to rear a child who was "nice to know." Wanting that and only that, I survived the early "just you wait" crowds, the boring, self-regarding parents who knowingly predicted that my child would be no better than theirs even though what theirs were becoming did not seem good. Sooner or later, they thought, what they perceived as a house of cards would come tumbling down around my ears as my child began to deal drugs or use everything from fashion to fentanyl as she abruptly threw herself into opposition to the tyranny that was her parents.

"Just you wait," they said as their towheaded fledgling cheerleaders "went out" with grammar-school boys, driven by their parents to the cinema where they'd sit in the back rows and rub buttery popcorn fingers across each other's parts.

"Just you wait," they whispered cautiously, thinking I hadn't heard, as they smiled approvingly upon their daughters' dressing in clothing that became scanter as the girls grew older and fuller without growing "up."

"Just you wait. You'll see what happens," they'd say when I began to give my daughter the choice of $100 or a birthday party with other girls she didn't enjoy but felt obligated to call friends. To change it up, I sometimes offered a trip to the science museum and lunch out for her and a friend, followed, if she wished, by a sleepover.

"That's okay, Papa," she would say, comforting me in my uncertainty.

One mother was particularly incensed when I allowed her to go to a birthday party but then—at my daughter's confidential request—picked her up at 10 p.m. instead of letting her stay the night with the gaggle of invited girls and boys.

"She'll be lonely," said Arleigh's mom, peering out from the heavy door of her marital loneliness. "She won't have a lot of friends." The dull man who was a tad Todd stood behind her shoulder, nodding thoughtfully while wondering where he'd left his car keys.

"How many friends can one person have, really?" I asked. Sure, in our mindless Twitter and Facebook age, we count anyone willing to befriend us as a "friend," knowing full well that they are not and that when push came to shove they'd as soon throw us under the bus. Who wants those kinds of friends?

My daughter didn't. She didn't even like Arleigh, really, because Arleigh was so much like her mother. Though my daughter never would have said as much.

I was grateful for her other friend, Margaret, who to me seemed so much of a rag doll, so seemingly lacking in imagination and engagement, amenable to all things uninteresting that while she served as a friend for years and years, eventually the root of the friendship could no longer nourish the spare and fruitless branches.

Still, I worried. The "just you waiting" caused me to sometimes wonder if I was right. I watched. Took her to the park in the evenings, told stories about our favorite Squirrels, animal stories that connected her to my grandfather and the ways of the Human Beings. Now and then I even dared to ask her if she was happy to which she answered me she was. We took her to London, England; Dublin, Ireland, where I taught summer school or, in the summers when I didn't teach, to the museums and foods, the cities and towns of Italy where generations ago her mom's grandmother was from.

Perhaps this is another moment to digress and remind you that when I was younger, I thought I never wanted children. Having children hadn't been a good fit for my parents, and it seemed important to ensure that the string of unfitness be snapped or cut by not having children. Neither of my sisters did, although one might argue surrogacy in

the way one adopted her Chicano students and the other adopts everyone, from graduate students to incarcerated Natives. But—a "just you
wait" warning of my own—if you think you might not want children,
then do not marry into an Italian family. It doesn't take a good deal of
foresight to know that have a child I would. It would take foresight and
a sense of after-humor to admit to what I became the instant that baby
daughter emitted her first cry. I made visiting friends wash their hands
at the sinks in the maternity ward, following them down to watch them
and be sure they did an adequate job. I felt annoyed when our closest
(then and now) friends joked about how our newborn daughter looked
an awful lot like John Tower—the first Republican senator from Texas
since Reconstruction—though I now marvel at how the infant John
Tower turned into the wise and beautiful daughter I feel lucky to have.
I batted old ladies aside at the Ubermarket when they leaned in to peek
beneath the swaddles, fanning away dead skin cells and the tricklish
dust of talcum powder with my hand, and should anyone threaten the
perfection that was my baby daughter, I drew myself up to the hulk of
harm and growled.

Needless to say, in my fatherly protections, I wasn't fun. And the
idea that children could end up like the wild Irish kids in the Dublin
close we lived in terrified me less because of their sneak-thievery and
more because of the feral way they traveled in packs that caused my
daughter to stare. More than one parent had told me just to wait, that
my daughter would not always be a loner like her father.

Once home in Michigan, I continued to worry. The packs of Irish
kids troubled my daytime and nighttime dreaming. Would my daughter throw over the enjoyment of being alone? Would she want to form
a club with Arleigh and ignore Margaret, and would they become as
nasty to others as I saw Arleigh be? Would she do things I wouldn't
want to know about, or would she go on walking and talking to the
park as we had done for years?

I worried that she would not have friends or have too many, like
most kids. Until the afternoon I went up to get her after "quiet time,"

the two hours that replaced the former naptime, when she could do whatever she liked as long as she did it quietly in her room.

I knocked on the door and went inside. There, I was surrounded by six or eight Paper People, three-foot-tall cutouts, drawn and colored and stapled over stands of cardboard so that they stood up. My daughter stood among them. With all the lovable seriousness of a young child, she introduced them to me one by one, describing their characteristics and personalities, the pleasures they took in talking and belonging, as she served them tea and scones with clotted cream and told them stories, which they then began—using her voice—to tell to me. Stories that led to more stories, as stories will, stories that calmed my worries and let me see in my heart the young woman and mother she has become, saying, "I am one of those people who is able to be perfectly happy with what she has, not sorry for what she does not have."

MOBY DICK

Must be the name, I am thinking as I watch towheaded boys enacting the rituals that will lead them to fraternities and into financial advising, trophy wives, and a fixed look of self-importance. I've come from a meeting, the senior silent member of the Promotions and Tenure Committee in my academic department at the local U. We review a three-year window of teaching evaluations, publications, and service to the department and university, each category ranked and then multiplied by the rating of the area to obtain a "merit" score, which then gets translated into a dollar amount for the smallest raise the university may give a humanities professor.* The process makes Bumpa grumpy. He reads everything he hasn't read before—much of which is unforgettably unmemorable—and tries to be fair but honest about the merit the teaching or work deserves. Three hours a day, three days a week, evaluating fifty-five faculty. The only break comes on the day you yourself are evaluated and you have to leave the room and stand in the hallway like an ill-behaved schoolchild, summoned back into the room without comment or question, if the downward glances and avoided eye contact are not comment or question enough. Bumpa is known to say, when a particularly grasping but lazy student asks how he might do better (by which he means improve his grade), "Go back to kindergarten and start all over, and this time pay attention."

Teaching evaluations he takes with a grain of salt. Why should the unlearned and sometimes unteachable praising or damning professors be taken seriously?

As for publication and the journals in which we publish for no one to read, one junior professor had written a tract damning Melville's

---

* Fair disclosure. My university treated me well and, on balance, fairly.

Moby Dick, and Bumpa was forced to sit there silent while the more vocal and certain committee members talked about why Melville was so despicable. Evidently, it was the phallus.*

But of course had they actually read—read as in read the words in a forward, hegemonically Western direction—they'd realize that Moby has no dick.

For that matter, these days in America most men don't either. Most men are almost categorically "dickless."

Take the ones who wear wifebeaters and, by treating women with an angry, even violent disregard, maintain the illusion of dickiness. They might be dickheads, but they sure as shootin' ain't "dicked" or even "dickey." Being an asshole, being a violent asshole, neither confers nor confirms masculinity. Violence toward a woman (and dickheads are usually woman-specific, exhibiting not "violence toward women" but brutality aimed serially at one specific woman) conveys nothing more than stupidity, irrationality, and a general frustration at the feeling of being a Castrati who has no voice.

It is frustrating to have no voice, to feel as though no matter what you "feel," nobody cares. Watching television—what Stephen King calls "the glass teat"—raises in frustrated boys-men a strange fantasy of a fateless Oedipus Puer, boys who would be kings by nature of their violent boy-ness—these voiceless develop and exhibit a certain je ne sais quoi, a polished balance of asininity and mulishness as if from mother's milk, a glowing inhumanity of commercial television and the lying producers that fund it.

This is, of course, initially what excused the rock-solid 30 percent of voters who voted against the apparently liberal establishment. They watched Fox "News," and Fox "News" allowed them to feel left out, ignored, and vulnerable to Russian meddling, "bots," and other acts of war. The liberals didn't help, calling these people "deplorables" and ignoring the one thing that American voters seem to care about, the economy and jobs, the pay for which allows men and women not only

---

* I know you don't believe it. Neither did I.

to support their families but even to find a little left over for fun at the end of the month, which is why the lower-middle and lower classes are so susceptible to the promise of tax cuts. It doesn't matter if the rich are saving millions. Not really. No one wants to sit around the Formica table and say like a schoolteacher that there is not enough money. Like D. H. Lawrence's "The Rocking-Horse Winner," there must be more money, and an extra $150 a month counts as long as you don't recognize what the potholes in your roads are really costing you in car repairs. And Fox "News" does not mention—ever—that President Obama didn't just save jobs but saved the entire country's economy, which had just about gone to Jesus when he entered the White House and was forced to alter his hopes and changes to focus on that, and he succeeded.

It is more frustrating to have a mind, and feel as though it may not express itself, which is why even the educated or thoughtful find it easier to watch the NFL than observe the causes or solutions to ISIL, easier to talk about "outcomes" as long as outcomes are jobs and jobs bring in money, which after the point of necessity means the ability to purchase more glass teats to suck on. Entertainment replaces culture, and in the world of entertainment, what Vargas-Llosa calls "massification" leads to quantification and reification. What follows reification is self-concern, self-regard, a narcissistic attention to self. And, as Gogol's narrator warns us in "The Overcoat," we end with "every private individual consider[ing] all society insulted in his person."

Or her person. For if rumor is correct, then we no longer are to refer to "him" or "her." I had a young woman the first day of class get angry and drop my class because she was more intent on her agendas than on the life of the mind, which, as Plato tells us, requires "purging and rekindling." She wasn't interested in purging (unless she would by that mean bulimia), and even if she had a match—and she was peerless—her kindling was soaked in Stalinism.

It is easier to make assumptions and to act and write about those assumptions. It is easy to be shallow and thoughtless; it is equally easy to be a person of diversity and massified of colors; it is becoming easy to "inhabit" a "space" in which all words are descriptive and all descriptions are bad if they don't agree with our own. (Evidently, it's all too easy to use quotation marks to indicate question and disagreement.) A shallow liberal or conservative substitutes his or her own brand of silliness for the self-righteous, fascist silliness of the not-her or not-him.

Picking on the so-called base conservatives is easy. All you have to think is that stupidity, willful or uneducated, is funny. You may laugh at their wifebeaters or orange comb-overs or eyes that are pale compared to the tanning bed of their faces. They don't even know the words, let alone the rhetorical methods, for reading *Moby Dick*. For them, it would be no more than a weight to hold in place divorce papers, nondisclosure contracts, and Klan hoods on the stool they use as a desk.

Picking on the liberals seems harder—well, not really—but a lot more fun, if only because like the satirist who joins us all into the embodiment of something laughable, the picking includes picking on myself.

My topic thus is birthed.

Really? Birthed? As in conceived and carried to term and then squeezed out like a bowling ball onto my foot?

The forty-page anti–*Moby Dick* tract spent the first five pages telling me how the project, of which this agenda-ridden tract should be seen as a culmination, was "birthed." I imagined a departmental meeting of chickens: an academic hen struts among us all, scratching about in the fallow dust of what once was the humanities until, with a squawk and cry halfway to peacock, the hen stops and pushes and pushes and lays an egg upon which she then sits, warming it to birthing.

In the midst of this "scholar's" unfertilized eggs was the angry idea that Richard Pryor ought to have a statue erected in his hometown. With a prostitute mother and a pimp father, Pryor is a Black man who told it like it is, but because of his Black-ness and his parents, he has been denied the very important honor of being memorialized with a statue in Peoria, Illinois.

Peoria? Honestly? Was Richard Pryor—besides being a very funny comic in New York City, admired nationwide—if not worldwide—concerned with the absence of a statue of him? Did he think all of society insulted in the unerected insult to him? There's no statue (that I know of) to Betty Friedan—also a Peorian—whose narcissism reached way beyond Pryor's to an entire generational gender. Somehow the lack of a statue means that the birthing hen of this article is, being also Black, "erased." As though a statue of Pryor would be equivalent to a statue of her, and its absence an indication of intentional erasure.

This concept of "erasure" somehow arrowed from Richard Pryor to *Moby Dick*. It's a movement as tangled and circuitous as the posters of human intestines on my doctor's wall. She hated *Moby Dick*. And in this Pryor case, this woman was Black and thus, attentive mainly to herself, was doubly indicting of Melville and his novel.

Granted, there are no African Americans in *Moby Dick*, but there is the noble, good-souled Queequeg whose skin color is no whiter than the African incarnation of *The Confidence Man* in Melville's novel of that name. And why would a ship setting sail from Nantucket to hunt whales necessarily carry along an African American, particularly an African American woman? The *Pequod* doesn't carry Betty Friedan or her great-great-grandmother either. Does that mean that feminists are "erased"? No Natives, no Latinos or Latinas, no one resembling the Afro-Caribbean Usain Bolt, and as far as we know, no Serbians or Croatians. All, I fear, erased.

But there were Africans in America when Melville wrote *Moby Dick*. Okay, so why don't you accuse Hawthorne of erasure as well? Is every writer supposed to cast about him or her and include every race, gender, and creed in his novel? Kind of loses narrative flow and pace, and besides, isn't that what's called an encyclopedia?

Part of the method of a novel or story is selection, choosing the right people, the right actions, the right environment and surrounding details to make a story in which readers engage and from which they learn, well, something. What gives a critic, any type of critic—and their theoretical categories are legion—the sheer chutzpah to insist that this novel or that story should have had this or that character in it? If a novel is a created world, invented to offer a truthful process, then are we to reverse the Gogolian sentence and tell writers that all truthful, invented worlds must include in their selected societies all people?

And are these not falsehoods in themselves, these insistences on "all kinds" of people? Are all Black women alike? Are all Indian men alike? Do people, regardless of race, creed, or gender, not fall in and out of love, marry or divorce, sit and read good or bad writing, think, feel empathy or sympathy, have children, rear children, get sick or well, care for others who get sick or well, purge their complacent notions and rekindle their ideas, the frameworks for their perceptions? And do novels not contain, as James Wood suggests, details that seem meaningless until we realize that they—the barometers on the drawing room walls—are exactly the kind of thing that we would expect to be on these people's drawing room wall? Things, in other words, that have no symbolic or metaphorical meaning but do have realistic meaning?

And is not realism the broad umbrella beneath which all other literary-isms shelter?

So you want to write a novel in 1851, a grand novel that instantly demands some limiting of scope. You pick a whaling boat because on a ship, once you leave port, the number of characters is not only limited, but also an automatic hierarchy of characters—captain, first mate, harpoonists, cabin boy, crew—exists. The crew is the crew, the way townspeople are the backdrop to a few selected characters. Their color or race is hardly subject to treatment other than to let us know they exist—they row or raise and lower sails, we assume they urinate or defecate, sleep or work in the long disconsolation that is workaday life, argue, and even fight. One of the crew could have been a Black man; but in 1851 is it likely that one of them would have been a Black man? Wouldn't a man not subject to slavery or a man who'd escaped the indignities and evils of slavery not have better sense than to ship out with a Captain Ahab in a ship barely larger than your modern bathtub in search of a whale the size of Nantucket?

Would the gold doubloon have been enough? That reified hint at commerce and greed and gain that is supposed to (but doesn't) lend value to the search?

Would a statue have been enough for Peorian Pryor?

JOY

Dear Bean,

I never wanted children. Or so I thought as I passed like a Field Mouse through the Rattlesnake of my thirties. Childhood was painful and seemed like too much work for the strangers who called themselves our parents. We made unreasonable demands upon the resources of an unhappy household. Like asking for cooked food to eat, especially food that wasn't burnt by my mother's bitter unhappiness and seeming regret at having married the confused man who was my father.

Then I had one. A child. Your mother. Well, *I* didn't have one, your nana did. I mean really, men have a little too much fun and then pay the penalty of watching their lovers balloon to the size of a Goodyear blimp, motoring around ever more slowly, inexorably heavier and clumsier and wearier until one day, wham!, her contractions come more quickly, and they rush in several different directions, one to find the bag she packed for the hospital, the other to find his keys and wallet. All the time guided by the birth-giving woman, they lever her into the car and take her to the hospital. There the men wait uselessly by, retrieving ice chips or resting on a foldaway cot. Maybe making telephone calls.

In this moment, men are just that necessary.

We, your nana and I, attended all the birth classes. We took pillows and sat on the floor and tried to do things the bubbling instructor (who'd never given birth to a baby herself) said. A few of the moms, sans dads, seemed sad and trapped by the addictions of smoking or poor eating. Their opposites, the trimmed and coifed and kept moms of athletic clubs and gyms, accompanied by salt-and-pepper neuterites who acted as though they made a lot of money and were thus merely slumming for the benefit of the group's appearances, gave little snorts of surprise if we tried to talk to them. We tried to enter the general well-intended spirit of the therapeutical group-talk and failed, your nana because she feels privacy is a state of being, your bumpa because he cops to a shyness that is more likely a form of wanting to be alone and left alone. When some bot calls, if Bumpa doesn't recognize the name and number, and sometimes if he does, he simply lets the voice mail pick up any message, knowing Nana will check when she gets home and tell him that he might want to call X or Y, which he may or may not do depending on his mood.

The birth classes went on for weeks. Every Wednesday evening, we showed up dutifully carrying pillows and products as requested by the instructor, and we'd go through exercises that prepared us for the real thing, for that moment without equal for which many sensible people utter one word, "epidural," and maybe smelling salts for the poor suffering male. Having observed the real thing, I'd agree with the epidural crowd and find the natural birthers and their cohorts like the Lettuce People ("I eat nothing but lettuce") a bit like tyrannosauruses.

As for smelling salts, well, before I met your daddy who passes out at the sight of blood, I'd have said, "Grow up and do your little bit." But his suffering is real, and there is no controlling much of it.

Fortunately the birth classes, as in Louise Bogan's great poem, "Roman Fountain," reached to their rest and fell, ending in the image beaten out in mental bronze of a man standing uselessly, helplessly, by, unable to strive when striver was his way, as Nana pushed and pushed and let out cries of pain admixed with expectant pleasure and your mommy was born. A nurse handed me a pair of sterile shears, and *Ecco!*, I knew what a necessary man was to do. I think I made a rather fine cut in the umbilical cord as Nana sweated against her pillows, exhausted. Her expression changed from beatific and relieved to one of frown and fright as the nurses ignored her, ignored me, and began fiddling with the newborn on a heat-lamp table without even giving the swaddled lump of bone and flesh to Nana to hold. Helpless though I'd felt, extraneous as I'd felt, admiring the sheer courage of women who give birth, I felt more so as the nurses began tampering with your mother because something—and they didn't stop to tell us what—was wrong, something that turned out to be all right. Turned out that she had swallowed too much meconium as she tripped her light fantastic through the birth canal.

No one told us anything until Dr. Beamon reentered the room and, annoyed, a little angry, told the nurses to let Nana see her baby, and I saw what utter joy looked like as they laid the nine-plus pounds of your mommy into the crook of Nana's arm. At that moment, I knew what men were worth as the tears in her eyes washed me like a slippery liquid down the totem pole from *número uno* to *duo*. I knew I had a choice: I could work hard to be the best papa I could and regain some position without caring what that position was and whether it mattered or not; I could envy the life-giving talents of a woman and the bond that is formed not at birth but over the nine months of a normal pregnancy with all its pains and discomforts, fears and expectations, birth classes and baby books that render themselves almost useless in the birthing and rearing. On the other hand, I could resent it, somehow, and feel the self-pity derived from fake news and begin to seek a salve for my childish thoughts.

Nana handed my daughter to me all swaddled and red and wailing and small with her little head of matted black hair, and she gave me the one cross-eyed look that saw clearly the choices and made them for me: I would put aside childish things, overcome my own upbringing, and be the best papa I could.

Often I have wondered if this was my first feeling of joy. The first time ever in my life of real joy. Was that it? With an admixture of terror as I looked down into my daughter's scrunched up face with its misshapen skull and thought with the blindness of a new parent that she was beautiful. Perfect. Not like those other babies wailing away in postnatal storage rooms. And when Peter Valenti—an old, old friend and talented ceramicist—joked that she looked like John Tower, I confess to having felt annoyed and perhaps a little angry at his humor. The fact that now, thirty years later, I am able to look back at photographs and see that indeed she did look a bit too much like John Tower seems to prove to me how much broader my joyful humor has grown. By now, thirty years later, that baby, your mother, is perfect in so many ways: wise, intelligent, beautiful in spirit and person, and she looks as little like John Tower now as I believed she did then. I may stare at her until my eyes lose focus and still I cannot see the John Tower in her. Not any longer.

And which is joy? Then, thinking her perfect is probably (thank heavens!) what all new parents do when they aren't texting or shopping on their mobile phone or distracted by boredom or the girl or boy in naked tights slithering through the mall.

Is joy then, with the breathless weight of sudden responsibility (what have we done?) and determination (we'll find a way, if we don't separate, divorce, or murder or die)? A stepparent is not fully and completely a parent at all, because even a strong bond of love lacks the permanence of holy heavens, this peeing, pooping, burping thing as it grows and reveals its character is me, my sister, my mother, my aunt, my grandmother—whatever portal the genetic pressure pushes open and out like lava from an active but stable rupture in the rise and fall of the surface of the earth.

Or is joy now, when the molten magma has cooled into the eddies and shapes of lava rock that one may look at and mnemonically remember? Does that make joy nostalgic? Does joy come sometimes after long cooling periods? Or is it only joy in the moment: the moment that does not, in reality, exist since all moments may be noted and spoken of and thought about only after the fact, like the telling of stories, which is why the present tense is so misleadingly false—it seems immediate, but it has not the frame and balance, the depth and lift, of the narrative past; it is all unconsidered passing into what will be past enough to evaluate, like an infant who becomes a girl becomes a young woman becomes as delightful a human being as your mother—the once and never future John Tower?

There are moments of joy, momentary joyfulness that fills you with the relief of love as when your mommy—she maybe six or seven years of age—walked, her small and fragile hand holding my gruff one into Glendalough, south of Dublin, Ireland. I was in a mood, though trying not to show it, when, without missing a beat or a step, she said, "Don't be grumpity, Papa," in a voice that sounded, indeed felt, like an angel singing, and I laughed, the cares and worries of the week sliding off my back into a pile of denial: "What? I'm not grumpy."

And London days, when arthritically condemned to the double-decker bus while you and my family walked, you waved and then sang to me when we remet about the wheels on the bus going round and round, or the times you danced through the back door wearing your new pink Crocs and showed me how balletic they allowed you to be, pirouetting on your very tippy toes as I held your hands for balance, or days in between when you snuggled into my ribs and we watched *The Nutcracker* yet again, and this old, solidifying nut case remained cracked.

Whether walnut shell or hardened lava, the worst thing for an older person is to become frightened and begin to see conspiracies everywhere like the true believers of state propaganda, whether on North Korean news or in the mean, cruel lies of Fox "News." Seeing department stores as trying to take advantage, or Exxon Mobil as nefarious and cheating, or fantasizing that tax cuts mean anything to anyone who isn't in the top 10 percent while farmers and Union Pacific workers lose income and jobs. Is it joy that keeps an older man from those absurdities, from actually thinking it reasoned to say and possibly even believe (though I have my doubts) that the "March for Our Lives" protesters ought to do something practical and real when we all know that what Rick Santorum is shilling for when he says such things is no more matterful than Chuck Grassley's saying that the social safety net allows the poor to smoke and go to movies. They're just kids, Rick, something evidently you never were and your cognitive abilities never got beyond, and disciplined, articulate, self-possessed kids with something important to say beginning—beginning—with protest and demonstrations of the massive support, kids we ought to encourage and, like Obama, say to, "We're glad you're here," and "We've got your back."

Crack the shell, Rick. It'll hurt, like the burn from the early levels of Dante's hell, but it may allow you some feeling akin to joy if you escape the Inferno. And remember, joy is always mixed, at moments occurring almost as an "aha!" moment after indignity or pain. And remember, too, given your professed Christianity that suffering—as in "suffer the little children"—means "allow," and they are coming unto to you, not becoming like you, and they may find your honesty and greed and venality wanting and say, "BS."

Forgive me, Bean. As you can see, Bumpa is a somewhat serious person who doesn't do joy easily. Indeed, he wonders if he is like other people, other men. Though he suspects anyone who claims gender as an excuse or motivating reason for anything, given how there are women who act and think like men and men who act and think like women; who wouldn't want it so unless they long like academic "humanists" who inhumanly want everyone to feel and think and even dress alike? He is always looking for the more that isn't said or used as evidence: a woman complains that women aren't treated equally in his academic department by their very excellent and competent (woman) chair, and he wonders, "Why?" as well as "Why not?" when really he ought to wonder "How?" and "How not?" The whys are difficult. If the complainant hasn't published in a department that has bylaws giving weight to publication (except for the Sunday church bulletin that one of the old and wretched and often wrong men claimed should count), the question of why seems easily answered (though not, evidently, if you're one of the women who assert discrimination, which is one reason I value having a woman chair—the former male chair was always open to accusation and criticism, even though I found him fairly fair, mostly fair, though not always—and he was and is my best friend in the department and has done me untold good). The how is another thing: she is given a platform from which to speak and argue, and she should be given it, though if I ever have to sit silently listening to a never-publishing Chicana colleague lecture us on how all the university is insulted in her failure to accomplish anything, whether in service or publication, I will retire.

Oh, that's right. I am retiring.

But then I have always been retiring. I've tried to speak in favor of junior professors as well as for the replacing of part-time instructors with tenure-track assistant professors (the difference in salary alone is staggering—which is why the U likes part-timers, even though the education given and the experiential expertise is so minimal as to make these hardworking but not exactly competent people powerlessly "enslaved"). In response, I have felt as well as seen the odd disregarding looks of my more polished unretiring colleagues. I could claim it's because I, too, qualify for discriminatory assertions, being male but also Native American or Indian, neither of which term is accurate, there being no "American" when my grandfather was being Native, and India being a place Columbus couldn't have hit without wings to lift him westward over the Panamanian isthmus. Come to mention it, Columbus never even hit the land mass that is now called America.

I was retiring long before those looks. For example, when Gigi Tincher raised her pert little breasts and complained to our balding eleventh grade English teacher that he had given us too much homework and I said, "Grow up, Gigi, and do the work assigned," I got sent outside with my desk to sit on the lawn and "think about being nicer" by Mr. Breault, whose little hands were simply stiffened by those pert breasts and the lilting voice of the girl who wore them. As I watched planes pass over the horizon, north toward San Francisco or west toward Japan, I did think about it, and I decided, "Nah. If you are going to speak, you ought to speak as truly as possible, and what I said to Gigi was as true as I got." So I retired, did my work, and only rolled my eyes when Mr. Breault's hands went stiff over Gigi, poor Mr. Breault who was so pathetic he wouldn't qualify as a target for #MeToo-ism.

Retirement, observation, being (I hope) better in writing than in speaking, taught me that joy—the joy of the airplanes overhead, a miracle of engineering and physics—is always mixed with the drones of complaint coming from the open classroom door behind me. The joy of freedom is mixed with the bell of tardy if one is late to Miss MacNamara's Latin class, where Charles Bacon—who got a D— scored nationally in the top 1 percent of Latin-taking students. Miss

MacNamara's reply if you said you didn't finish your translation from Cicero was, "I don't understand. You understood that I assigned it?" Looking back fifty years, I think now that she truly did not, that her not understanding was not a rhetorical response aimed at making you feel unretiring, but a genuine and authentic expression of her world-view. It was assigned. A student's lamp stayed lit until the assignment was completed; Caesar ordered you into battle and you raised up your shield and fought. Imagine the momentary joy of a compliment from Miss MacNamara as opposed to high praise from Breault, similar to the joy I get when a student survives my criticism and finally "gets it," and the getting shows in her or his writing. A joy that is mixed because my retiring self will miss my own teaching, while my imagined retired self will enjoy the freedom.

And that's the truth of joy, Bean. It's passing and to come. When we say that someone is full of joy, or always joyous, we think, "Yeah, full of mindless joy," which is not joy at all but unevaluated thoughtlessness or religious ecstasy. Indeed, joy is fleeting. Perhaps when one has enough moments of recognized joy to connect them like dots in a puzzle, they make a picture of contentment, something of which I've had more than my fair share.

Joy itself comes and goes, and when you pirouette into the room in your stiff pink Crocs or bow yourself off the balletic stage, I feel it, I know it, and I am grateful that I had children and my children had children.

Should it remain in the room, it is no longer joy. So I let it leave, and with that I am content.

The Hydra-Headed Question

Sooner or later it had to happen, Bean's question, "Bumpa, do you believe in God?"

The answer, of course, is "no," though ever since moving to the Midwest and buying a house down range from Catholic chimes across a small forest and large park, where the parishioners park their cars and SUVs aimed outward, evidently for quick après-Mass escapes, I've learned to mitigate my "no" with "Sorry, I know it's hard to believe, but . . ." as a way of avoiding too much contention with people whom I generally appreciate if not like.

After all, a Catholic exiting Mass is usually unarmed and not particularly dangerous, though in these days of America's sinkhole of -isms—race, sex, religion—and a "president" who is a narcissistic racist, gyno- and homophobic name-calling child ("Did too," "Did not," "Did too")—one may never be quite certain, given how so-called Christians are more likely to shoot themselves in their morals by voting for a pedophile. Catholics seem much like gay men who never in my life have seemed at all threatening even when hitting on me; indeed, the gay couple down the street is known to have loaded a generator into their BMW SUV and driven up and down our block looking for people in need of emergency power during a stormy outage—good people, both, although evidently not good enough to be accepted at any church other than the catch-all Unitarian one downtown.

I don't mean to make fun of Catholics or Unitarians, gay people or straight. I admit there was a time that I was dead certain about my atheism, seventeen years old and in a seedy Dublin pub late at night singing along with songs I didn't even know were the folk songs of IRA supporters. I just liked the songs and the lilt of Irish tongues forming a cloud of community in the still nighttime air in the age of Mountbatten. The same way that I liked the songs like "Onward

Christian Soldiers" that we sang on Sundays in my father's Southern Baptist church and the thoughtless hum of community as I went with a busload of never-to-be-dangerous youth groupies to Hopi land to dig trenches for water and sewer pipes and do general refurbishments to Hopi hogans.

But the wind blew and blew and like the mud sealing the hogans' log frames, the seal of the songs dissolved into the realization that while the community felt good, for me it was false. The mud dried and cracked and fell out, letting the cold slip in like T. S. Eliot's fog on little cat feet that were clawed. Suddenly I realized that I felt uncomfortable around all these good-feeling youth. Not unlike a Black person might feel in a group of White friends, or a White person might feel among the rapid-fire, story-making tongues of Latinos.

It's hard to believe it had to happen. The question. Most of us don't spend our days worrying over whether there is a God or not, and only when we need it do we stop and consider: Should we vote for an alleged pedophile, or ought we to expect people in power to behave with moral superiority (or at least equality) to us; if God is testing Oklahoma with another batch of tornadoes, is believing in God more than a way to accommodate the pain and suffering of the victims? Would anyone in his right mind invent such a windy, capricious God to believe in?

For that's what one has to do: believe. You may not prove or disprove the existence of God; you may only maintain your Faith in him or his son even while marking your ballot for utter immorality and sin and hope for God's eye to be too busy with the sparrow to notice the divarication of your commandmental faith. How else is a conservative Christian going to allow himself to send death threats to the University of Alabama's field-goal kicker for missing a game-winning goal? Or, in my personal case, a woman who after declaring herself a good Christian, told me that I ought to be killed for saying something that even to this day is nothing if not true, that "to remember that if you want to be x, you have to be x," meaning that if you want to be Midas, rich and able to turn all you touch to gold, you have to live with the fact that you are excluded from the common realms of humanity.

You may with algebraical aplomb substitute for *x*.

You may say that there are good and decent people who are Christians, and you'd be right. There are. Like Republicans who these days find it hard to admit to being (or having been) Republicans, these Christians are caught between the tenets and subsequent actions of being Christian and those who justify close-mindedness with their claims of being Christians. The point is that if you claim to be a Christian, then you have to think and behave like a Christian. You have to *be* what you say you *are*.

I said it about Mitt Romney, a fairly moral man, when he ran politically against my preferred candidate, Barack Obama, an honorable, moral, and decent human being. You could put Obama into the Romney sentence as easily as you may put Coyote: remember, if you want to be a trickster you have always to be a trickster capable of tricking himself with his cleverness—something that seventeen-year-old in a Dublin pub should have known, but didn't.

Yet.

At seventeen, life kind of just goes along and, when you aren't whining about living in the richest most privileged country in the world, seems, as a friend would say, "copacetic." Suddenly, if you are paying any attention (and these days most people pay no more attention to things than the limited data and screens of cellular phones), you are questioned: about place (what are you doing at or in *x*?), about faith (in what *x* do you believe?), about purpose (what are you doing and why are you doing it?).

The evangelical patient in the hospital bed beside me, behind the curtain dividing our double room, told his sister that he felt sorry for the people who did not know where they were going, because they had no purpose. He was a considerate roommate, which to my way of thinking was a good roommate. He insisted on asking his friends and family, to whom he kept bragging about the surgeon's saying that he'd never seen a prostate as large as his, as though an enlarged prostate were the red badge of courage, to be quiet or not telephone after nine o'clock to avoid disturbing me—a humane kindness that one rarely sees these days as the driver at the short light in front of you finishes her texting before dazedly looking up to notice the once-green arrow is now yellow and runs the light to leave you waiting through another interminable cycle of red, green, and yellow without seeming to notice that she is not alone in this desire to move, to progress, to advance toward a predetermined goal, toward a limited here-and-now purpose.

I often know where I am going—Macy's or Sansu Sushi or the golf course. As for the kind of purpose evangelical Scott meant—joining Jesus in Joseph and Sons Carpentry, LLC—I am not so sure. Does he really believe that when he dies his worm-eaten corpse or Ziploc bag of ashes will in some *Star Trek* fashion be beamed up to a place where Jesus exists in body, able (with God's help) to reconstitute his ashiness into Scott the Believer and carpenter's helper?

Evidently Scott does, to hear his sister and him debate over speaker-phone with a well-wisher named Darren—appropriately a carpenter himself who fucked up a table for Mrs. Dolittle by cutting six inches off the wrong end—whether or not Jesus made mistakes like that.

It's a curious debate, and lacking purpose as Scott thinks I do, one I'd love to join. Not to question or challenge their worldview or their seemingly calm belief in Jesus as friend and neighbor, but to say this: if Jesus was real and actual, if Joseph taught him to work wood well, and if he never made mistakes, then I would not be interested in meeting or knowing him.

Horrified at times by my own failings, my own mistakes (remember the Black and Tans entering that pub fifty years after Easter 1916?), I don't trust anyone who has never made mistakes. Worse, I find them inhuman and boring. Consider Dante's vision of Paradiso: a multifoliate rose stepped around the center of light singing Hosannas. Really? True, the Inferno would be less than desirable, in part because of the popes who inhabit it, and Purgatorio would be much like the middle third of a long car trip across Nebraska.

But right outside the hot of Hell—on the earthly side, in that First Circle of Limbo—is that area that contains all the interesting people of the world who were not Christian—Aristotle, Plato, Socrates, Saladin,

Avicenna, Averroës, Lucan, Ovid, Horace, and my all-time favorite, Homer, the singer of tales that make and shape the world. "Sing in me," Homer says, "and through me tell the story of that man skilled in all ways of contending," the tester extraordinaire who unlike venal modernity wants to know the shape and firmness of the ground before stepping onto it; if you're a feminist, you have the wise and affectionate Nausikaa or the heroine of heroines, Penelope, who is able to fend off the most assiduous of sexual harassers (who, not unlike the Harvey Weinsteins of the world, are silenced justly in the end).

If I believed that after death the rotting cells and organs that once were me survived together and went to a place, that picnic ground outside the entry gate to Hell is the place I would want to go, to listen, to be, to think and discuss and maybe, if someone will listen, tell a tale or two of my own.

I had a friend in high school—Art Troyer—who asked me what Bean is fated to ask me, and when I said, "No, I neither believe in God nor in a physical afterlife singing or woodworking or just excluding from my church everyone who is not agreeable to me or who with the callow error of youth misses a field goal," he laughed and replied that he believed in God because he figured it was safer. If there wasn't a God, then no harm, no foul. But if there was, then he'd be admitted to heaven.

"I figure that if I try to be the best person I may be, then a just God will recognize that and at least let me hang out with Homer," I continued. "Besides," I thought, "I don't really want to spend eternity shooting pool with hypocrites like you."

Art and I weren't, needless to say, close.

Eventually, I decided that one's afterlife was not in catching a flight to ether land. It was in the memories and love one left behind. In one's daughter or son who, being loved without qualification though with guidance, passes on the tale of you to their children's children, honors you with remembrances that may be told happily and well, unlike my own poor father and mother. For each of my parents, I feel continuously sorry and regret that I am unable to find any other feeling than sorrow outside of resentment, which I have been trying to overcome for much of my imperfect life. Resentment does not allow for interesting or educative stories, and Grandfather along with Homer taught me all too well that only stories that instruct and capture the imagination, allowing for the participation of the listener or reader, are worth the trouble and effort of production. One doesn't just hope but works hard to ensure that the stories told of him or her after they have completed the dust-to-dust cycle are interesting and founded in and on love. Chekhov's "Heartache," love; I. B. Singer that most humane of writers, love. Even Burgess's *A Clockwork Orange* is, in its way, about love.

But Art Troyer was not about love; he was about getting (he was, after all, White American and eventually, I suspect, venal Republican, like Charles the Chucklehead Grassley or Orrin Hatch, interested in getting tax cuts at the expense of CHIP and the other social safety nets like Medicare and Medicaid and Franklin Roosevelt's Social Security, which allows my elderly neighbor to live with a tinge of dignity, that distant expression of love and respect for human beings less fortunate). As with my parents, I feel sorry for the homeless Republicans like David Brooks or Steve Schmidt, the moral people with whom I might disagree, carefully. Very carefully—and "care" is related to "love," which carries the burden of respect—re-*spectare*, looking again (and again) with regard.

The afterlife for venal or foolish Republicans like Hatch and Grassley could be to join the usurious or immoral popes in Dante's Hell. If only. Hatch is very nearly there, and Grassley is grazing his way ever closer. Worse than a lifelong burning would be to be around those two for all eternity: at least Roderigo de Borja, Pope Alexander VI, had some fun, although these days he would be forced (and rightly so) to step down because of his treatment of mistresses. But we may take comfort in the idea that you cannot resign from Hell.

It is this that I want to convey to Bean when she asks if I believe in God. I will begin with questions: Do you want to have the unhappy expression of a troll and the narrow-minded inhumanity and utter stupidity of Reagan's "Cadillac welfare mother" or say things like "A poor welfare cheat spends his benefits on cigarettes, booze, and movies"?

Movies. Really, Chuck?

Do you want to be forced to sit in endless meetings with decrepit Orrin Hatch—all men who claim that they once were poor, as though that explains or justifies anything—like having one Black friend or claiming you're not anti-Semitic by saying one of your lawyers is a Jew? Do you want to watch cable news for eight hours a day and wear an orange comb-over and complete the ruin Reagan began to bring, changing America from a republican democracy to a helpless hopeless oligarchy by trickling all over the people who do not receive the benefits from tax cuts for the wealthy?

Bean's answer will be "no."

And I will be content as I teach her that hell is not a place; it is a process. It does not occur in another life. It occurs now as you lose your ability to understand that there but for fortune go you and I, or that the important thing about money is to have enough so that you don't worry about buying decent food or paying your mortgage or rent, or giving your kid a bicycle for Xmas. If you're a troll who thinks poor people simply want to take advantage of the welfare safety net you are trying to destroy, then besides foolish, you have never felt the real discouragement that comes from working and getting paid too little to manage and therefore needing help from not your government but your neighbors by means of government, and you have never wanted to explain to the checkout clerk at your local grocery that you work but that you really do need the food stamps to supplement the afterlife of the vegetables and fruits you cadged from the dumpsters behind the supermarket.

"So, is there a god?"

With a smattering of humility I realize that for thousands of years people have wanted there to be a god. A god "who provides," as though God is a kind of cosmic Santa instead of a meditative wall that one reaches as one considers life and death and meaning, although if a troll's life were to be taken in a corny midwestern tornado I might think that god had some beneficial agency but still wonder why God has not taken all of the self-righteous hypocrites who might actually vote for a credibly accused pedophile and run them out to sea in leaky rafts.

"I don't know" is the only answer I can give Bean. And here is where I begin to win the argument she does not even know we're having: if there is such a thing as an afterlife, then it is in the words and stories that our children and children's children tell. We live and are loved beyond our earthly years in those stories, in those good things people remember about us.

This doesn't place us at the center of things. Rather, it does the opposite. It melds and merges us into a broader, longer passing of time. It is not without its relation to what a true Moslem or true Christian or true Buddhist seeks, which is a relation to eternity. But I lack, and the traditions of the Nez Perce lack, a full or real understanding of what the word "eternity" may mean or be. Swallowing Monster does not begin or end. Coyote does not begin or end. Either may be told as story, but given eternity, story does not begin or end except as a matter of management or convenience and what we are to take from story—Christian or Nez Perce is not "what" but "how," and that how-ness does not exist along a line but, like water in an endless and endlessly sustaining well, "small" hows exist and temporarily mean. We are only small embodiments of those meanings. Again, temporary except in the one way eternity exists for a Nez Perce, in story. To exist in story means you have to behave in a how that causes people to want to tell the story—for a granddaughter, for example, to want to tell her children and her children's children how Bumpa was and, out of that "was," be able to create a different was, which is "would have been," a would-have-been that is not just possible, probable, and believable but that is true. Thus my problem with the common usage of the word "fiction." Fiction is not something made up out of whole cloth; it is the whole cloth of Truth with a capital "T." Ultimately, it is humbling: you do not ask "How should I be?" but rather "How would one—a Nez Perce, a Christian, a Moslem—be if he or she wants to be one about whom good stories get told?"

You, Bean, believe what you will when it comes time to believe. Ask yourself if you really want to hang out forever with the grim-faced joy of an evangelical singing hosannas to a ball of light. Or would you rather be there with the greatest—the Homers, Saladins, Platos, and Averroës—telling stories, finding justice, trying to discover not to conceal, agreeing and disagreeing, making mistakes, being human, and having your son and wife stand with you as you clean your house of immoral men?

So maybe God does provide. He provides the sadness that is Orrin Hatch and the sorrow that was my father. And he provides the Bumpa who intends for Clara Bean to believe what she needs to while she remembers him for as long as she has memory and words. And believe me, she has buckets of words . . .

I'VE BEEN DEAD SO LONG
IT LOOKS LIKE LIFE TO ME

Clara Bean, as you might imagine after the death of Stan Dards who was wiped out so easily by a brand-new Dodge Ram truck driven by a remedial driver distracted from crosswalks by texting, had questions about death and dying, and the assumption—and gratitude for my taking it on if the relieved semi-smile on her father's face is anything to go by—that I know a lot about Death is not incorrect.

I've met him.

Death.

He looks nothing like a skinny, faceless reaper in flowing black robes. Indeed, he looks like nothing more than a surprise, a change-able surprise not unlike the Confidence Man in Melville's novel of that name, who invites and allows people to take advantage of their selves, to cheat their selves due to their own ill-gotten motives. Death is sort of like that: he—and without meaning to sound politically incorrect, I've always thought him a "he"—lets you go along like Coyote until you are lulled into inattention and, whoops!, you fall into the cre-vasse or are gobbled up by Swallowing Monster and you find yourself enclosed in the moist, churning darkness that is the Monster's stomach.

When you come to inside that stomach, you have three choices: submit, make the best of it, or find a way back out.

Now, I am no more given to submission than Bean is. Someday, though a good deal more likable than I have ever been, she may con-sider herself a bad colleague, unable to sit in a department meeting and listen to coworkers go on and on about agenda and practice, telling us all like an unstable Lazarus come back from Mar-a-Lago.

Of the other two, making the best of it is a choice that comes third, not second. First, you try to find your way back out, gathering the Assiniboine and Gros Ventre Indians already inside the monster's stomach, build a roaring campfire that causes the monster heartburn, and then when he belches, toss more and more of your new friends out the opening of his gullet, diving out at the last second before the belching ends. You could go out the asshole, like Dante the pilgrim did, led by Virgil through the Circles of Hell, but that's really for Muskrat who loses the fur on his tail as the asshole puckers shut. Humans are better off with the gullet.

If that doesn't work, then you have only that third choice: it is by far the hardest choice, but it never supersedes the attempts at the second choice.

Since I was not supposed to live at birth—Clara Bean knows this because it is family legend—I have been stuck with the final choices, the penultimate and ultimate choices, which change according to the belly of the beast in which I find myself. The initial choice, of course, being an infant and of an age that is as preconscious as college freshmen, I was seen as submitting. Who knows if raising my little fists and shaking them at the blurs behind the translucence of the oxygen-tent coffin I was in was not submitting but issuing a challenge and promise—or to my poor mother, a kind of male-determined threat. For Mother's relations with males, including her own son, were complicated and cold, not unlike Father's relations with women and his own children.

Regardless, from the moment the doctors let me out of that oxygen tent and sent me home to the happy place with a sliding roller gate keeping us children out of the living room, where my sister's turtle was not found until the winter when the furnace roasted his rotting corpse in the floor vent and the smell pervaded the hallway, and where my other sister, chasing me down the hallway into the bathroom, discovered the fragility of a wall mirror on the outside of the door as I slammed it in her face (thank heavens she was not injured, though much surprised), I was two things: (1) determined and (2) a Sartrean existentialist who believes in choice even when the individual seems incapable of choosing or the choice seems no choice at all, a baby who grew up believing that Death was not Someone or Something to fear, but a part of life that gave life meaning.

I've sought out metaphors for this meaning. Mark Schorer, the literary critic, said that the thing to do upon finishing a good novel was to reread it. Immediately. I recognize the rightness in this because it is not until we reach the novel's end that we have encountered the wholeness of its structure and the apparent finish of the process in which we have been engaging for however many hours and days. Only then, knowing the end, may we go back and reencounter those processes and understand them more clearly. In the case of a novel like *One Hundred Years of Solitude*, we may reread and reread again even after we realize that with all that begetting in the beginning and the revelations of the destruction at the end, the one hundred years is a record of human existence as large in its way as the Christian Bible's Genesis and Revelation.

Somewhere long before I read *One Hundred Years* for the thirteen times I have read (and four I have taught) it, I realized that life is a process not unlike a good and fully written and well-told novel—if one's life is good and fully and well told. It is not about living in the moment, despite what the athletes and shrinks tell us ad nauseam. It is about seeing the moments as part of a process, the end of which you may predict because you have had sufficient experience with analyzed living processes to see into what is the opportunity, possibility, or probability for what may become or be.

It is the relation between the life's effective title and the opening sentences. When Graham Greene's "The Invisible Japanese Gentlemen" opens with seven Japanese Gentlemen at a table in the corner, you know—you *know* (because they are immediately made visible to you, the participatory reader)—that they are invisible to someone and that that invisibility will tell us all, in this case about that particular someone's "powers of observation," which are touted but humorously nonexistent. If Dylan Thomas's "A Story" opens, "If you can call it a story," you know again, but this time that you should not look toward what happens and the results of that, but to something else, that it is not a "Once upon a time" story, but simply, a place and the characters who go with it.

We hold dear the image of a man's life passing in front of his eyes at the moment he dies, and although that seems to have been reduced to a man's Twitter feeds passing across his cellular screen, the question arises, Why? Where did this passing come from and what meaning do we take from it?

Chicken and egg, of course, given my literary sensibilities, but probably what we mean by it is that at the very end of our lives—just before exiting through the door of conscious being to wherever we imagine we're going or through the Dantean gates of Hell, which is where hypocrites who talk about the debt burden on our grandchildren after passing an unnecessary tax "reform" that benefits the rich at a prosperous time when taxes should go up, not down, so we may reduce that burden, enter to join the wonderful murderers, usurers, and simonists, the corrupt popes of whom there have been more than enough to populate several circles of the Inferno—we look back in survey to measure the good and bad processes along with their results and take stock of the "goodness" or "badness" of our lives.

In my own case, that reckoning will include lots of shitty things I did as a fifteen- to thirty-year-old male, some in relation to women, others in relation to men or the public weal at large. After those ages, however, it will also include the presence and existences of my children. I always wanted to overcome a terrible father and frightening mother, nearly collapsing in front of a lecture to seven hundred students the day I heard—I heard in timber and tone—the preachy certainty of my father's voice come out of my mouth. Nonetheless, I will go to my dust more happily knowing that with constant awareness, attention, and work, I managed to be the "papa" and "daddy" that my respective children call me. As proof, I would show you how they are in the world. As additional and final proof, I would show people the continuation of the generations that is represented by you, Clara Bean.

For that is what that final assessment is about in part: How do you or I fit into that ongoing context that extends seven generations before us and for seven generations to come? How have I bridged from there to there, from past to expected future, and have I been a good and strong bridge, or have I left the connection damaged, rusty, threatening of collapse? And how will I know?

I won't. Because what I would know are the stories that you tell of Bumpa, fed, begun, encouraged by your parents, your uncle, and Nana. Essentially, then, when that moment flashes before my eyes, what I will suspect is whether the stories will be good ones told with love and humor, or stories that are bad, which are inevitably forgotten like the unimagined thoughtless stories of weaker creative writing students. I can remember their good ones, or many of them; I barely remember their bad ones a half hour later, when I reach toward my rest and home. Only that their bad ones all look alike, shallow and without that ongoing awareness of the love of words and language.

Not knowing when that moment is, well aware of the moments that have already happened, means that I have to live as though that moment could be today, tomorrow, or next week. Not dissimilar from the way anyone else ought to be: don't, with smallness of mind and lack of humanity or love, let the day pass without telling the people you love that you do love them. More important, don't let an instant go by without letting them see in the way you behave that your love for them is constant and continuous. Don't be so surprised by unexpected dying. And don't be all about Me. Be about Too. For that's the danger of our important moment in history, that #MeToo will become about the "Me's" without the communal, attitudinal change of the "Too."

To get to "Too" demands living in Unknowing. It's fun, if you're up to it. I never know what these essays are about until you say something or do something that triggers the fading embers of my imagination and an idea comes along and tells me what the essay must be about. Words begin to follow word, sentences, sentence, and the process of making begins. It may sound mystical, but it is not.

Unknowing is not "not knowing." Not knowing is ignorance or the kind of sorry stupidity that is represented by the belief that 140 characters on a Twitter feed can convey more than name-calling or a bald-faced lie. By definition, it's a lie because it uses few characters to form fewer words that form less than one complete thought. I won't even mention nuance. That is ignorance, and ignorance breeds anger and childishness and impulsively releases false words into the sewer of lies. There is no collusion between lies and shit, only an eventual flush.

Unknowing is openness, an openness to discovery. A lungless baby placed in an oxygen tent to die peacefully who yet somehow lives has little choice but to live with unknowing. He has no choice but to learn to begin stories and essays with nothing more than the foggiest of ideas about where they might go and what they might reveal, and he knows that at any moment the end could come—and believe me, he was aware of that even in his dickhead years—and thus he keeps one eye focused on the possibility of opportunity, of turning expected death into life, knowing something of what life looks like and why we keep on trying to do it.

Retiring into the
Weir of Words

Words, like names, have power. They describe, define, and analyze. They express both surface and underlying intention and meaning. They don't merely tell us something, but they tell us who is telling us something, and if we pay attention or if we know a bit about the person speaking or tweeting (such as he is a compulsive liar), we may speculate with reason about the meaning beneath or behind the words. They indicate processes—the processes you use, whether intelligent and logical or dumbfounded by Fox News or ESPN. The words you use reveal to others (if they are paying attention, as so many are not) a little of who you are by revealing to the word-sensitive a lot of how you are.

It's one reason for literature: the more you read, and read without agendas, such as "There are no strong women in *Moby Dick*" or avoiding in our endemically racist country the word "nigger," as in Huckleberry Finn or Conrad's *The Nigger of the Narcissus*, the more able you are to recognize why a senator from Oklahoma is dodging the all-too-easily answered question about separating babies from their mothers and fathers who have risked life, limb, and all kinds of comfort and happiness to get their families away from an environment of murder, repression, and the violent hopelessness of gangs in beach communities like Puerto Cabezas, mothers and fathers who seek the chance to be contributing honest, decent, entrepreneurial, law-abiding, kind, and maybe Catholic citizens of the United States of Immigrants and Native Americans—because the senator himself could have been, would have been, kept out by the building of a silly border wall that will now seek to keep out descendants of people who once possessed large swaths of the American Southwest and West.

The words and names tell us something: San Diego, Las Cruces, Rio Grande, Colorado. And a good deal of the non-Spanish names are derived from the varying peoples called Native Americans. The senator uses words that go as far as possible to tell us as little as possible; the process reveals his lack of logic, intelligence, and his complete denial of immigration, one of the most important things that made America a great beacon and representative of responsible freedom and the liberty of processes.

Now you, Beaner, may remember me as the bumpa who asked every day even before your newborn eyes could focus on anything beyond your nose, "Can you spell 'Homer'?" I picked Homer because whether Euro-centric or not, he is *a* if not *the* master storyteller.

I will always remember you as the three-year-old who, seeing the white Puma on my Costco sweatpants, asked me, "Bumpa, what's that a silhouette of?"

My college students have trouble pronouncing, let alone knowing the definition of, the word "silhouette." Homer, I suppose, merged into the shadow beneath the "Bumpa was silly" umbrella you adopted, which was fine, although silliness is only the way we make what is a serious process (words and their use) less of a burdensome lesson and more of a recognition of connection, you to me, me to you, and us to the world around as you learn not simply to manipulate words, to use them, but also to enjoy the using (and once you could speak, you did not stop, even at times speaking audibly when you were sound asleep, as though like Frederick the Mouse you already were a poet or, if not a poet, were poetical with a poet's love of the texture and tone of words, though your love of words now seems to take a second place to ballet, and thanks to the miracles of technological reproduction you have danced the lead roles of more ballets than your bumpa knows).

Aside: Poetry derives from the Greek "poiein," which means "create," and thus every human being who creates is, like it or not, poiein-ic, although most people nowadays think of poetry as metered verse that has little or no relevance to the getting and spending of their consumptive lives, in which financial literacy seems more to the point than literary literacy.

"Can you spell 'Homer'?" is not a joke but an admission that stories are everything to someone whose entire life has been spent manipulating words: from the young boy who negotiated his mother's and his father's anger, which could turn violent on a dime, to the solitudinal teenager who ran for senior class president and surprised even himself by winning, given that he was known to think the opposite of what people believed he thought—or ought to think—to a young writer who was arrogant enough to believe he was the best writer in his fiction workshop at Syracuse University, to the one professor in the creative writing program at Michigan State who believed that creative writing should not be taught as much as rhetorical reading and thus assigned every semester a course pack of short stories that he changed up only to keep from becoming one of those professors who repeat themselves to meaninglessness in their ebbing, leftover impassionateness (Dylan Thomas's story is titled "A Story" and opens, "If you can call it a story"—why?), knowing as time and circumstance continued to reduce what students learned before they arrived at university to look stunned inside his classroom that he'd get in response a dull timidity from students who were preoccupied with disguised, unspoken interest or a genuine absence of any passion for writing and literature worth reading. By people who aspired to be writers.

Ah! Bartleby! Ah, Humanity!

Does anyone wonder that Melville's Bartleby, though a copyist, was a scrivener? Does anyone wonder why John Cheever said that he often copied out the first pages of published stories that he liked? Doesn't the student who skips "The Custom House" preface to *The Scarlet Letter* miss part or all of the point of the tale? And surely there is something amusing about Henry David taking up residence just outside of Concord, Massachusetts, on land owned by Ralph Waldo Emerson who brought him food and supplies and checked up on him regularly? But then there is a similar amusement to *Tinker at Pilgrim Creek*, which was written as I understand it mainly inside a library at Annie Dillard's "reserved" carrel, just as there is a joy and happiness to establishing a relationship with that force we call "Nature," which is caring, positive, informative—a process of ultimate processes, regardless of how or where the writer who "keeps the inmost Me behind its veil" of the making of that relationship and who, as Hawthorne claims, puts "myself in my true position as editor, or very little more, of the most prolix among tales that make up my volume,—this, and no other, is my true reason for assuming a personal relation with the public."

The "why" in Thomas's story is several-fold. It tells you that either the writer is a fool who knows not what he does or how he does it, or that he is the opposite. No one in his right mind opens "A Story" with an immediate assertion or question, "if you can call it a story." It also tells you that this story is not a story like most stories with plots and developments but that it is "about" something else that happens but happens to reveal, not to develop; it is about a boy and his uncle in a context, revealing the characters who go on an annual pub crawl along with the aunt who tells her loud and "trumpeting" husband that if he goes he need not come home, while he both goes and comes home as she knows he knows he will do; it is about a boy going along on this pub crawl even though he will have to wait outside the pubs for the men of legal age to enter, drink, and exit, again, each time louder and more revealing of their characters. It leads the reader who is paying attention to suspect that this writer knows exactly what he is doing and prepares him to revel in the writer's details and words—and Dylan Thomas is a master of words and details, reason enough to read him over and over and over even in a story that seems to come to nothing. Seems, because "A Story" is a story a lot like life itself.

The Hawthorne whom Hawthorne invents—the "editor" of the tale of *The Scarlet Letter* reveals, if we are paying attention, something more. Many things more. Hawthorne did not leave "or very little more" in his sentence because he was trying to achieve the word count required of an English class student essay. Rather, that phrase reveals the addition to the possibly creative and important task of editing, the editing writer, the man who is playing with words in such a way as to both tell the tale and reveal both framework and interior purpose—the precise process that "The Custom House" is managing for the tale itself. It offers a measure of the truthfulness of the tale: this may not be fact as the mundane mind understands it (the mind that thinks casually that a table is hard and not in subatomic motion or that America stops being good only when it tries to be great, just like a person who wants to aggrandize himself when it is others who aggrandize a public figure for what he does, not for the lies he tells by calling truths "fictions"); but it is true.

Just as history—the real learning of that large framework of civilization for the past two thousand–plus years—provides a context in and through which to see the movements of peoples, their art and architecture and culture—literature—stories in which the writer is a very little more yet a necessary little more than the editor of a most prolix tale—says to us that in these situations or contexts, this is how a character behaves and these are the substations on the way to dying that he visits as he remains believable, probable, and possible. History lets us decide who we are and how we want to be or to change being; literature lets us imagine who we might be or what we might come to if we act this way or that. They are equally important and highly related, and both well done are equally true. "The Custom House" suggests—gently and only on rereading suggests—that assuming a relation with the public demands great care and caution, and that while one wants to edit a true tale, one ought not to aspire to stand out in the "tale-ing" because it is not about "you," not about being famous or rich, but about managing the words. Always the words. And not to impress, to get people to admire you, but to express, to say what needs saying how it needs to be said.

There are lessons, here, Bean. One is that the story may not look like a story in a conventional sense, but nonetheless, the words and the characters expressed by the words matter. You may substitute "life" for "story," and the truth behind the words and characters remains similar, if not the same. Characters who are careless about the words they use—and these are legion—tend to be careless, reckless; people you may enjoy may ask if there is such a word as "reck." The person you so lovingly call "Uncs" or "Uncle" asked me that question and the echo of Old English allowed me to say immediately, "Of course there is" (you can't be careless without care being a possibility); in Old English the word "reccan" means to take heed or have a caution and an engaged, enjoyable person should always have a caution about the words he uses. Treasure such a person, whether as a friend, lover, or acquaintance, and remember, in your distracted digital age that just because someone claims to have two thousand "friends" on whatever internet platform he uses, two thousand friends are not worth having and the kind of energy and intellectual and emotional engagement required for "friendship" will always mean that you may have—truly have—no more than five or at most ten "friends" (if you include family, as you do already), and while the rest encircle you with words, most of them encircle you with meaningless or reccan-less words and thus their lives, if you may call them lives, matter only in the sense that you will not interfere with their enduring them.

And that brings us to the second lesson (it is one reason we read, or should, and why we ought to want to encounter Old English as well as any and all foreign languages because of what it tells us about other peoples and how they engage with the world, which may be interesting and thought provoking and to no more purpose than that) and that may be learned from Virginia Woolf or the great Elizabeth Bowen or the Graham Swift of *Waterland* but here is represented by the embodied narrator of "The Customs House." When you, Bean, assume a "personal relation with the public," "keep the inmost [you] behind its veil" not to dissemble but to edit, to make sure the tale you tell is interesting and as true as the context and character and words will allow, and the goal of which is not to aggrandize yourself or impress your audience but to allow your auditor/reader to engage in a process that will reveal as much of and as close to the truth as may be gotten from words—structured, contextualized, consistent, reccaned words. And remember in this relating to keep your inmost you behind its veil—no one who is honest will claim to care about the daily trials and tribulations, the joys and celebrations of the isolate Bean. Those may be shared with your five friends and family who were present and engaged, but beyond that, the sympathizer is probably thinking more of him- or herself, his or her agendas and generalized confessional self-pity than of you. When he says, "I know what you mean," he doesn't, and you will recoil from his assertion of knowing, realizing it to be a cloud of unknowing, a generalized, self-involved assertion that he, too, has suffered—whether more or less hardly matters—without knowing that "suffer" means not merely to endure but to allow.

Unaware, linguistically reckless people will tell you that when you edit you are making a falsehood, which they will call a "fiction," revealing to you their recklessness and unimaginative thoughtlessness. For "fiction," to those of us who spend our lives doing it, is true and fact is friable, the hard surfaces of fribblers whose horizons of time have shrunk from the epical Kronos through the Horological and down the rabbit hole of Chronological to the immediate here and now–ness of Atomical. They live in the particular—the "particle-ler"—and as history is rarely taught or learned anymore they cannot understand that it takes an entire tabletop of particulars to make a surface on which they may rest their wearily confused numbskulls. They may want "change," and when do they want it? Now. When may they get it? Maybe in a generation or two. And even then, they will not have forgotten but never learned and thus never vigilantly protected the pitter-patter of change as it moved slowly forward, reaching a particularity that wants to modify Penelope, criticize Odysseus, and refuse to recognize that Telemachus is, indeed, and by his actions shows himself to be, Odysseus's and Penelope's true son or that self-aggrandizing breakers of customs and laws deserve little more than an arrow through the larynx.

Returning to Hawthorne, we can realize the master storyteller Odysseus is, like the imagined author of "The Customs House," a master editor who keeps the inmost self behind its veil. In Hawthorne, it is to further the tale, to give contextualizing, linguistic liberty to the editor of the prolix tales. In *The Odyssey*, it is often to disguise and protect the hero-self at least until Odysseus is sure of his context and sure that the context is safe for him and the stranger he meets, while assuring the public that he is not threatening to them—to Nausikaa's reputation and honor, for example. In this sense, a Yeatsian sense, certainly—Odysseus is a consummate student—one who studies, who discerns context and nuance, who understands what might be or might happen if x or y is revealed, who reccans his position in the process in which he finds himself and who not only accepts but also relishes his responsibility for his actions and the way in which they reveal him.

From dependence on "fact" to a belief in the processes of "fiction" was a direction I always wanted to take students, away from what other nonwriting professors (I mean novels, poems, stories, literary essays, not criticism, though there remains Mark Schorer and some less than well known critics at second- and third-level colleges and universities who have written some pretty interesting essays in language that someone like me can understand, essays that reveal and do not hide ideas like fleet-footed rodents from the night-hunting owl) have taught them: that this is what this novel is about. To take students from "about" toward "These are the words, and you must pay attention to the words and figure out how they mean whatever they mean, and we may talk about it if you have the interest and the passion for those words and not for your careers or your training or the sometimes false measure of your grades (which has become the collegiate version of 'money,' as in measuring a man or woman by how much money he/she makes)."

A novel—which is why I always had trouble teaching novels—is not "about" something. Like life itself, a novel is a journey, a process that modifies and changes page by page or chapter by chapter, and it must be reread and thought and rethought about, if it is worth the effort of reading at all. A novel is not "subtle" in the sense of disguised or difficult to ferret out the meaning, though it may be "subtile" with its connections and contexts shifting and changing the flex of the spiderweb's strand that we are momentarily following until we branch out onto another strand and it folds back on the first or extends the first in a different direction, or it adds to the feel and fine of the emotional complex in which we find ourselves. But to find ourselves in any emotional anything requires us to feel words, to hear them as though they are spoken to us or by us with much interest and sensitivity and awareness that comes from an expanding history of reading.

I have loved the word "subtile," with an "i" in it, since I first read it in a seventeenth-century poem. (Was it Donne? Marvell? It could have been Herbert or Milton.) Or did I come across it in *The Canterbury Tales*?

It took me years, decades to realize that as a writer (or person) you may need to be subtile for your own pleasure but that the pleasure should not show. The telling, the process, should remain clear to the reader and only if he goes back and wonders as he wanders through your prose might he—might he—glean some of that pleasure for himself. But it should not be a necessity of the first or even third reading, not a necessity at all, but merely an enhancement of that "personal relation with the public" that the "very little more" establishes.

Now, in my opinion, all good writers have these subtileties. All good writers have to have some fun, and writing a story is work, but writing a novel is serious work, work more tiring than teaching school or mining coal. Faulkner wrote because he could not find the prose he enjoyed, and believe me, Faulkner unedited reveals a mind so complicated as to be almost impenetrable at times—and we, the public, are always seeking a sense of the mind behind the words, aren't we? His opposite, from my point of view, is Hemingway and his simpler, short sentences, and when Hemingway is good, he is very good, representing the other side of American prose from Faulkner, the side that lets Raymond Carver be as good as Raymond Carver is when he lets us feel that we, too, are caught up in these mysteries, these unarticulated situations, racing toward ends that are only more confusing and subtile, sticky, difficult to separate and define. One step—or sometimes one word—too many and what we take to be ineffable can turn shallow or clever, a cliff edge that Ray seemed always to walk as carefully as one may walk a cliff's uncertain crumbling edge.

Take, for example, my use of the ad hominem attack word "saltines," as in "cracker," as in a salty White person on either side of the Mason-Dixon Line who supports such kindnesses as separating infant Latinos from their mothers and fathers, or "tax reform" that leaves their towns and cities and parishes without the resources for education or roads or healthcare or public transportation. (Why have public transportation? Well, if for no other reason than we need the hardworking poor to be able to get to their third shift of the day.) As for healthcare, providing affordable access to it is not a right, unless we want to have a civilized community of diverse and varying people in which we actually care about the well-being of one another. Though I am fortunate to have healthcare provided by my employer for life, my neighbor having healthcare makes my block, my neighborhood, my county, my state, and my country more whole, more complete, less anxious, and I don't need to meet a stranger and worry that an illness is going to wipe out his savings, if he has any. It's selfish, really: I may feel content, and better than content in the knowledge that affordable access to healthcare actually may save money for hospitals and clinics by reducing the sheer amount of emergency care.

So "cracker" is selfish, and "saltine" is barely better except for the fact that most people would not—and who might expect them to—get it.

But to be aware of this, one needs enough education in literary fictional or historical words to read and understand my journalistic heroes: Paul Krugman, Joyce Vance, Steve Schmidt. Phil Rucker was, too, until he lost his hero status by speaking of "untrue facts" the other night, indicating that somehow in his dispassionateness he has succumbed to the notion that there is a thing called "fact" that is "untrue." Phil may regain his status easily, by admitting that a fact is a fact and is, by its facticity, true, though possibly useless without the other atoms of fact surrounding it. Otherwise, it's a falsehood, a lie, whether intentional or not. For a "fact" to be "untrue" requires a surface and an underpinning—not unlike conspiracy theories—and Phil in his words succumbed to the American disease—dis-ease—of relying on the surface appearances rather than the underpinnings.

Beyond—and to me and you, more important, add in the literary heroes. Take Homer, Boccaccio, Dante, Milton, Aristotle and Plato, Shakespeare (obviously), Chaucer, Keats, Wordsworth, Wilde, Bowen,

Woolf, Swift (Jonathan and Graham), Greene, and Memento Mori both in title and in expectation, Twain, Faulkner, Melville (but not really Stephen Crane, namesake of a fiction prize at Syracuse), Heinrich Böll, *Njal's Saga*, Chekhov (leaving out Chekhov would be akin to leaving oatmeal out of your granola), William Trevor, Tobias Wolff (who is at moments brilliant, though not too well known), and then add the poets Thomas, Roethke, Bogan, Yeats—always Yeats—and you may begin to experience the ineffable nuances of being alive, and a playwright or two like Yasmina Reza (*Art*). Add in J. B. Priestly, Dylan Thomas (whom we reread every Xmas to the once children and now their children), Mary Blue (Nez Perce), and Bill Bryson (*Notes from a Small Island* is without question wonderful for the Angophile, and I remain that), and the seven different dictionaries (one the compact *OED*, which takes effort and a magnifying glass to read) and *Elements of Style*, name dictionaries, and dictionaries of slang and unconventional style books, and you find enough pleasure to last a lifetime, each pleasure leading to more pleasures as well as to a rereading and reconsideration of pleasures already taken, like the mental memories of journeys taken on which you may not go again. But then you may not, or should not, reread as though recapitulating a journey taken, but set out anew again, as openly and as willing to discover what you missed the first or second time, which proves that novels are not "about" and reveals to the rereading reader how *Life on the Mississippi River* eddies and changes and that Marking Twain may occur where you never expected it to occur.

With all these and of course many more, you may begin to see through the surfaces of "fact" to the depths of language and relational context, and if someone does not read or does not value reading—every day or night—then avoid them the way you would step around grave markers in a graveyard of the existing and not living. Don't judge them, just stay apart from them even in their company, and try not to be overcome by pity. Imagine being a man who doesn't read. Imagine being a man who is dull to deadness and maybe because he's never grown up with art (or because he's never grown up at all) is essentially evil, and certainly always wrong.

For reading, like living, is a gerund and gerunds are processes that are necessary to being in the world. And remember, Bean, it's not a matter of knowing the word "silhouette"; it's a matter of wanting to know the word "silhouette"—just as it isn't a matter of being rich in resources but being happy in the richness of your family, community, country, and ongoing times, your connection to the processes that make human beings and not simply protoplasm that occupies space—or, in the classroom, desks. Students who assert that they should pass the class because they bought the books. (And if you think that is absurd, which, of course, it is if you mean "ab-surd"—"out of tune" or "intensively deaf or muffled"—this has occurred in my forty-five years of college teaching more than once, and believe me, once was astonishment enough, especially when in both cases the respective deans decided to override my Fs and replace them with "passes" on a "pass/not pass" scale; but then what are deans but well-intentioned or greedy people—not the same things, always—who begin slightly deaf and become intensively deaf by being caught in the Platonic Cave's echo between departments and faculties and those pale beings called "administrators"?)

Unlike deans or administrators or literary theorists, then, you need not only to recognize that stories are that, stories that help you recognize the hows of the life, the doings and beings of life that make you a living human being, but you need to listen to and hear your own words and to think about what they are meaning.

With and through words, being a Being is somewhat ineffable and I say amen to the ineffable of human existence. Amen—"so be it"—a basic way to end a Native story or an immigrant's sermon and prayer. An essential way to end the tale of Bean or Bumpa because neither tale is finished yet, not quite, not ever, really, as the story of homecoming, the "Nostoi" continues beyond the physical fact of life itself and so as one travels through this process that we call life, one has always to be both declarative and creative, sustained and yet aware that opportunity lurks in not the situation but in the ways in which any particular situation may be responded to. I may be retiring, but then sometimes shy, sometimes content with solitude, I have always had a core of retiringness in me; to enter "retirement" is, for me, not possible—to wit, this book.

To see the ineffability of those ways, one needs the purified language of poets along with the modest relation to the public that Hawthorne reveals. One, of course, needs history because with history, one may not declare, "I give up," and throw his hands into the air and really do that, give up, because giving up, like Shakespeare's sleep, is but a picture of wakeless death.

I want you to be awake, unretiring, and never intellectually dead.

I want you to possess this weir of words.

ABOUT THE AUTHOR

W. S. Penn is a mixed-blood Native American (Nez Perce) who taught creative writing for forty-five years. He is the author of two novels, *The Absence of Angels* and *Killing Time with Strangers*; a collection of short stories titled *This Is the World*; and two collections of essays, *All My Sins Are Relatives* and *Feathering Custer*. He has won the North American Indian Prose Award, Native American Writer of the Year, Native American Editor of the Year, an American Book Award, a Critics' Choice Award, and the Stephen Crane Prize for fiction, and he has been recognized among the Best University Press Books (*Choice* magazine). Additionally, Penn was a Washburn Distinguished lecturer and has won the distinguished Faculty Award at Michigan State University. He has published stories, novel excerpts, and poems in numerous literary magazines, among them the anthologies *As We Are Now: Essays by Urban Mixbloods*, *Understanding Fiction*, and *Everything Matters: New Autobiographical Essays by Native American Writers*.